A Time to Clash:
Papers from a Provocative Pastor

Doug Giles

Copyright © 2007 by Doug Giles

A Time to Clash: Papers from a Provocative Pastor
by Doug Giles

Printed in the United States of America

ISBN 978-1-60477-400-9

All rights reserved solely by the author. The author guarantees all contents are original and do not infringe upon the legal rights of any other person or work. No part of this book may be reproduced in any form without the permission of the author. The views expressed in this book are not necessarily those of the publisher.

www.townhallpress.com

Dedication.

For my dad, a WWII vet, an honorable gentleman, an old school, hard working, God and Country loving father who taught me many things. One lesson he taught me that's pertinent to the liberals and their lies which I address in this book is this: Crap is crap no matter how you frame it.

Recommendations

"Doug Giles takes no prisoners. He sees how a posture of accommodation and being 'nice' has dumbed down the Church and our culture and put us on a highway to Hell. Giles is the best I know at getting in your face and provoking the response of radical commitment which will create the righteous change we need both in the church and in our nation."

- Seth Barnes, executive director of Adventures in Missions

"Dirty hippies and womyn beware: Doug Giles takes on everyone and everything with little time for hand-holding nicities or political correctness. If you're looking for a book that takes a sledge hammer to modern liberalism, defends common sense, and has fun doing both, buy A Time to Clash."

- Lisa De Pasquale, CPAC Director, The American Conservative Union

"Doug's the real deal. Love him or hate him—just don't ignore him!"

- Jim Gillette and Lita Ford-Gillette, rock-n-roll dynamic duo

"Giles says things you would probably have said if you'd thought of it first. But you didn't. He did, which is why he has a book and you don't and why you should buy it!"
- Greg Gutfeld, Host of Fox News Channel's, *Red Eye*.

"If our elected leaders could speak as courageously, boldly, and with as much insight and wit as Doug does, we wouldn't be in the mess we are in. Buy this book for everyone you know."
- Gregg Jackson, radio talk show host and best selling author of *Conservative Comebacks to Liberal Lies*

"Any man who is known and praised both by Ted Nugent and R. C. Sproul is a man we urgently need to hear much more from. Besides, I like him a whole lot too, but don't tell my squeamish friends. It'd be much too hard to explain."
- Eric Metaxas, author of the book, now a major motion picture, *Amazing Grace: William Wilberforce and The Heroic Campaign to End Slavery*

"Doug Giles speaks the truth . . . he's a societal watchdog . . . a funny bastard."
- Ted Nugent, rock star

"Doug Giles brings a sharp, humorous, bold and captivating style to communication."
- Dr. R. C. Sproul, distinguished theologian and best selling author

Recommendations

"For anyone that thought Christians come in one flavor, bland; get a load of Doug Giles. Doug is living proof that if the truth offends you, that's YOUR problem. The truth is SUPPOSED to offend you, that's how it lets you know you don't have it!"

- Brad Stine, Comedian/Author/Actor and Co-Founder of Godmen

There is a time for everything, a season for every activity under heaven.
A time to be born and a time to die.
A time to plant and a time to harvest.
A time to kill and a time to heal.
A time to tear down and a time to rebuild.
A time to cry and a time to laugh.
A time to grieve and a time to dance.
A time to scatter stones and a time to gather stones.
A time to embrace and a time to turn away.
A time to search and a time to lose.
A time to keep and a time to throw away.
A time to tear and a time to mend.
A time to be quiet and a time to speak up.
A time to love and a time to hate.
A time for war and a time for peace.

Ecclesiastes 3.1-8

A Time to Clash: Papers from a Provocative Pastor

By Doug Giles

Table of Contents

Introduction: There is a Time for Everything xvii
Chapter 1. We Love Pepsi, They Love Death 23
Chapter 2. When Blasphemous Homos Rip into Christians the MSM says Diddly Squat 27
Chapter 3. A Christian Can Be a Christian or a Liberal, but He Can't Be Both 31
Chapter 4. The Ten Commandments for My Daughter's Potential Boyfriends 35
Chapter 5. The Ten Commandments for Husbands 41
Chapter 6. How Wives Can Kill Their Marriage: Part One 47
Chapter 7. How Wives Can Kill Their Marriage: Part Two 51
Chapter 8. How Wives Can Kill Their Marriage: The Final Straw 55
Chapter 9. The South Sucks? 61
Chapter 10. I'm Not Homophobic; I'm Chick-O-Centric 65
Chapter 11. Anna Nicole Smith's Death Blamed on Global Warming 69
Chapter 12. The Teenage Casualties of Casual Sex 73
Chapter 13. America's Obsession with Stupid Sluts 79
Chapter 14. Anna Nicole Smithing 83

Chapter 15.	Gun Free Zones: A Mass Murderer's Wet Dream	87
Chapter 16.	Southern Fried Children	91
Chapter 17.	Let's Call God "Allah" and Jesus "Slappy White"	95
Chapter 18.	Christianity Sucks and Islam is Awesome?	99
Chapter 19.	Atheists Better Pray to God They're Right	103
Chapter 20.	Hey Atheists . . . Get Your Own Moral Code!	107
Chapter 21.	Why God Needs the Atheists	111
Chapter 22.	How to Shut Up an Atheist if You Must	115
Chapter 23.	Atheism: An Intellectual Revolt or Pelvic Rebellion?	119
Chapter 24.	How Not to be a Cho Seung Hui	123
Chapter 25.	10 Steps to Becoming an Effective Conservative Campus Hell Razer	127
Chapter 26.	John Edwards Might Be Full of Crap, but Our Enemies Are Not	133
Chapter 27.	Pit Bulls and Stupid Fools	137
Chapter 28.	Traditionalists Don't Wear ButtSmacker Lip Balm	141
Chapter 29.	The Islam-O-Fascists Must be Happier than a Pig in Fresh Mud	143
Chapter 30.	Teachers Should Pack in Case Students are Attacked	145
Chapter 31.	Eyes, Ears, Nose, Throat and Car Bombs?	151
Chapter 32.	Get Britney a Gun and Teach Her to Hunt	155
Chapter 33.	A Sanctuary for Demoniacs	159
Chapter 34.	It's Time for Conservatives to Take Comedy Seriously	163
Chapter 35.	Olbermann's Obsession with O'Reilly	167

Table of Contents

Chapter 36.	Larry Craig is not Gay—He Has Restless Crotch Syndrome	171
Chapter 37.	Our Honorable Hunters and the Pain-in-the-Butt Tree Huggers	175
Chapter 38.	Rosie and Khalid Sittin' in a Tree . . . K-I-S-S-I-N-G	179
Chapter 39.	Satan Takes a Little Nap After Dr. D. James Kennedy Passes Away	183
Chapter 40.	Help! I'm Being Nifonged!	187
Chapter 41.	Christ the Contrarian	189
Chapter 42.	Our Shrinkage in the Global War on Terror	191
Chapter 43.	Obama Wants Your Evangelical Mama's Vote	195
Chapter 44.	Avoiding the Date from Hell	199
Chapter 45.	The Feminists Will Not Like You Reading this Book	205
Chapter 46.	José, Can You See?	209
Chapter 47.	Death Becomes Them	213
Chapter 48.	An Open Letter to Illegal Immigrants	217
Chapter 49.	Go Beyond the Pavement	221
Chapter 50.	The Re-Texification of Doug Giles	225
Chapter 51.	Raising Boys That Feminists Will Hate	229
Chapter 52.	Can the British Still Call a Cigarette a Fag?	241
Chapter 53.	Tasty Christian Books for The Serious Meat Eater	247
Appendix.	The Cultural Acid Test for Pastors	253
About the Author.		259

Introduction:

There is a Time for Everything

—⚘—

"Be angry and sin not."

—From St. Paul's letter to the Ephesians, chapter four verse twenty-six.

Anger, like alcohol, is only bad if it's abused; however, if used for right reasons and in right amounts (as the inspired Psalmist once said about wine), it can "make the heart merry." Anger might not make you glad as quickly as a second glass of merlot can, but if channeled correctly, it will make you giddy about something you desire but can't get—until you get angry.

For example: say you're an unemployed, 38-year old guy who does nothing but sit on your butt playing video games, smoking weed, living with mommy and dating 18-year old girls *and* guys. You know what? You should get angry with yourself because you, clearly, aren't top shelf tequila. You do not have a life, and it should make you mad that other people are actually productive—unlike you.

Need another example? Say you're overweight. Remember what it used to be like to walk across Walmart's parking lot without having to be gurneyed to your minivan by a paramedic? Remember the joy of not being able to hide small toys and half-eaten sandwiches between the folds of blubber on your body and being able to actually see your genitals when you use the toilet? Remember those simple pleasures? You do? Does it make you mad that you don't get to enjoy them any longer? It does?!? There you go ... see how positive anger can be?

Folks, this righteous wrath not only works for personal improvement, but it can also change for the better all aspects of our society—*if* we'll get righteously PO'ed in a precise direction. And there's the rub ... Our neutered nation tells us it's a big no-no to get mad anymore.

That's right, being angry is forbidden in our currently castrated culture—unless it's something that the liberal thought police thinks you should be ticked at, and then you're forced to fume also or you're ... you're ... you're a ... a Nazi!

Nowadays we've been forced to memorize this mantra of postmodernism that being nice and accepting of anything and everything—even if it is utter, uncut and unmitigated BS—is our duty. And it just so happens that BS is the chief characteristic of our society these days; we're inundated with it but not supposed to be upset by it, which is convenient if you are its seller.

Because we have allowed "them" to program us to be nice and not heat up (unless, again, it is at something that upsets the Left), we don't even blink an eye when we see the base and the vile; instead we force a smile. What a bunch of crap we've been sold vis-à-vis this whole uninterrupted "nice" wave we've been told we're supposed to surf.

Today, people can do something appalling, say something contemptible and delve down the funnel exalting the lowest parts of humanity—and what's to be our response? We're supposed to say, "Well, alrighty then ... okey dokey ... have a nice day."

There is a Time for Everything

Why do we show mock civility toward things that mock civility? Well, because "anger is bad." And we don't want to be bad, do we? No, we want to be nice. We're supposed to be a chilled-out group of pleasant and complicit prawns who do the Miss America wave no matter what kind of insanity gets shoved in our faces, up our tail pipes or down our throats.

Well, as a free bird, I'm not buying the *capitulate-your-convictions* PC crack that our culture is currently dealing. As previously stated, anger ain't all that bad boys and girls, and being nice when you should blow a gasket can aid and abet that which needs to be slapped down. Can you dig it? I knew you could.

So what gets my dander up? What/whom do I think is a threat to the US and that for which it stands? Or stood? What do I get freaked over?

Well, there are several things me no likey:

1. I don't like our nation being threatened by Islamofacsists. I think they should die on their turf and on our terms. Yes, I'm not buying this "religion of peace" smack.
2. I don't like homosexuals publicly mocking God and Christ with their bizarre S&M/B&D testicle festivals.
3. I don't like what democrats have become.
4. I don't like people screwing around with my right to keep and bear arms.
5. I don't like traditional values being trashed.
6. I don't like folks who don't like America.
7. I don't like the slutification of our culture.
8. I don't like metrosexuality.
9. I don't like abortion. I say for every aborted child we BBQ a baby seal.
10. I don't like how our universities have become liberal madrasas.

11. I don't like the idea of 11 year old girls given birth control without parental approval by public school fools.
12. I don't like the fact that teenage girls can have an abortion via the public school system without their parents knowing diddly squat.
13. I don't like second graders being told to read and embrace homosexual literature and lifestyle.
14. I don't like our borders being violated by illegals.
15. I don't like Christians being trashed at every turn in the mainstream media.
16. I don't like gun free zones.
17. I don't like sanctuary cities that house illegal aliens.
18. I don't like the diminishing resolve I see in our War on Terror.
19. I don't like how culture is making the white male out to be the Antichrist.

This is just a smattering of things I think stink of which I feel no compunction to accept. Matter of fact, folks, I think we ought to get righteously outraged and challenge those with such anti-sanity sentiments everywhere they raise their hollowed heads. If we don't solidly beat the Left and their ideologies everywhere they surface, the things we love as traditional Americans are going to end up as relics in a museum in a country that resembles a Tommy Lee keg party.

What follows are 50 plus screeds against people and principles that I believe are detrimental to church, family and state. Tucked within my verbal invectives I also promote people, policies, principles, books, organizations and websites that will lead the God and America loving person to resources needed to rebuild our original righteous and robust spirit.

Hopefully, after reading my book you, the traditionalist, will be stoked to be more responsible and engaged as a citizen in the direction of our country.

There is a Time for Everything

After 9/11 I decided I wasn't going to spend my ministry on the sidelines of life naval gazing and choir preaching in a narcissistic Christian la-la land; if I'm going to live and work, it's going to be a life of clashing with culture coarsening zombies and their dense ideas.

Since that decision not to be a beholden and silent cow to ripe and foul secular folly, I've had the fun and good fortune to carry out my mission on both major TV and radio shows across the nation, through writing five books, as well as through my weekly column on the nation's largest conservative online news portal, Townhall.com. Yeehaw! Not bad for a former drug dealing, messed up redneck from west Texas. God bless righteous outrage.

Lastly, in all honesty, as much as I enjoy being the provocateur, I'd really love to not stir things up, to be sweet like James Blunt or Joel Osteen and live a non-conflict life with my family sipping lemonade and fishing south Florida's flats. However, sometimes the times demand that we put aside our smiley faces and "take off our gloves" and clash for the soul of our nation. I believe that time has come.

Doug Giles
Miami, Florida
December, 2007

Chapter 1.

We Love Pepsi, They Love Death

Y'know, when I see videos of young Muslim men slicing their heads with straight razors in a frenzied jihadic pep rally, then I see videos of our young pimps and thugs or our Queer Eye for the Straight Guy males and our Darwinian throwback Jack Ass 2 droogies, I get a real bad feeling. It's the feeling that if our civilian teens/twentysomethings were ever to go toe to toe with post-pubescent Islamic terrorists that our young 'uns would get hammered.

Our soft and stupid culture is setting us up to be no match for these Muslim youth who are being wet nursed in Islamic death cults, being fueled with Muslim madness in a land with zero economic opportunity and are feasting feverishly on a steady diet of Anti-American disdain.

Yep, all things being equal, I believe they will eventually clean our kid's clock if we don't get a pro-American, kiss-my-butt attitude back into our warp and woof. These radical Muslim boys who currently reside across the sea (and some across your street) are not your normal young men.

This is sort of a problem for me. Why? Well, once again, Muslim young men dig jihad, and our youth love hair gel, teeth grills and blue jeans that are 17 sizes too big. Al Qaeda operative Maulana Inyadullah put it succinctly: "(Americans) love Pepsi, and we love death." This is not some moody,

PMS phase Islam is currently going through. This is their MO.

I believe that if we, as a nation (especially young adults), don't toughen up a bit—and do it quick—that we're not going to have the long-term stuff to cudgel off these persistent zealots. As I begin to stare at my 45-year mark and try to see down the road regarding the land my girls and their kids will inherit, I begin to shake like Shemp when he didn't have any cheese at the real possibility of the end of this great American experiment.

I believe our increasingly effeminate culture doesn't stand a long-term chance in hell against Muslim mayhem—unless we beef up a bunch and get back some of the now-endangered American resolve. And that goes for every American—whatever your politics, sexual bent and musical taste. If we don't recognize and realign spiritually, physically and politically to stave off these death dealers, then within 50+/- years we will be another head on Muhammad's trophy room wall.

Don't believe me? Look across the pond. Europe is history as far as their heyday goes. With diminishing birth rates and a thinning of skin, it won't be too long before the EU is Islam's prison chick . . . mop head wig, lipstick and all. For a more in-depth and disturbing look into how Europe is cooked, get Mark Steyn's latest book, *America Alone: The End of the World as We Know It.*

Having run out of analogies, adjectives and time, let me put this to you in a song I wrote (to be sung to the tune of "Imagine," by John Lennon).

    Imagine there's no America
    It's easy if you try
    Just a big Muslim mess
    No Stars and Stripes to fly
    Imagine all our people

We Love Pepsi, They Love Death

Living as Islamic slaves.
Imagine there's no Country and Western
It isn't hard to do
No baseball or hot dogs
as far a freedom goes, we're screwed
Imagine all our pretty girls
wearing black little sheets.
You may say that I'm a doom-n-gloomer
But I'm not the only one
I hope someday you'll wake the heck up
And our nation will still be strong.
Imagine there're no possessions
That's the Muslim plan
No need for Ford or Chevy
A veritable Suckistan
Imagine all our people
Losing all we have.
You may say that I'm a doom-n-gloomer
But I'm not the only one
I hope someday you'll wake the heck up
And our nation will still be strong.

Chapter 2.

When Blasphemous Homos Rip into Christians the MSM says Diddly Squat
(Written September 29th, 2007)

Can you imagine if a group of Christians got together and made a photograph advertising their upcoming rally, and in that photo they deliberately went out of their way to tick off homosexuals?

What do you think would happen? Do you think the mainstream media would cover it? Do you think Katie Couric, Chris Matthews, Swill Maher and the other liberal curmudgeons would wade in and condemn the Christians and call 'em haters . . . meanies . . . or . . . or . . . something?

You and I both know these darling duplicitous Christophobic thugs would be on their TV shows screaming anathemas at Christians louder than Yoko Ono would yell if she accidentally knelt on her own breast. They would be on the church like a dog on a June bug. Like Rosie on a case of Twinkies. Like Bill Clinton on Hustler's 2007 Chunky Intern Issue. We would never hear the end of it.

However, what does the Main Stream Media do when the tables are turned and the queer crowd spits on the Christian community by showing a bunch of S&M/B&D mooks as Christ and his disciples in an advertisement for the foul end-of-the-world-as-we-know-it Folsom Street Fair this weekend? Probably nothing.

Yep, the MSM will, most likely, defend Folsom's unwholesome flotsam as freedom of expression, artistic creativity and a progressive step away from the puritanical social mores that have for too, too long frowned upon their dream of an annual Testicle Pageant.

For the uninitiated, what exactly did the way-too-creepy gay crew at Folsom do? Here's the poop (literally). You remember Da Vinci's painting of Christ, The Last Supper, don't cha? Well the Wizards of Odd, yes the marketing crew at Freaks-R-Us, decided it would be cool to market their "Street Fair" by replacing Jesus with some black/gay/S&M dude and then...*then*...swap the disciples out for a bunch of randy bondage boys and ... *and* ... (they weren't finished) ... switch the bread and wine—which represents Christ's sacrificial body and blood given as a ransom for man's sin—with a bunch of rubber-fisted dildos, together with a broad selection of other fetish crap made only for the fetid critter.

Unreal stuff, right here folks.

Y'know ... even in my drunkest and drugged-out partying pre-Christ days when I was a very bad guy, I was always afraid, as messed up as I was, of personally attacking God, Christ and sincere Christians. But that was just me. Hardcore blasphemy doesn't seem to bother this gay bunch much. But I digress.

Back to the media.

As stated, I seriously doubt anti-Christian MSM and their squawking heads will hold the queer nation's fingers to flame for this. Why, you ask? They love it. Look, anything that will whiz on Christ, goof on God and barf on Christians is completely cool with them. Yes, my friend with Mange Stream Media, as far as Christians go ... there is no closed season and no bag limit for these buggers.

However, if anyone picks on, makes fun of, or tells the truth about a group the Left has decided to love, well you better buckle up, boy, because it's going to get rough. I hope you have tough skin.

But this is nothing new. Everyone who loves traditional values and has a lick of common sense can see the biased, hypocritical, nonstop sputum that regularly flows from these loudmouths' cake holes. That's why their ratings are tanking and their newspaper sales are plummeting. Matter of fact, it's been reported that 90% of those who purchase liberal newspapers now are parrot owners who use their rags only to catch Polly's runny white sunflower-laden liquid stool.

Frankly, I don't care if you Folsom guys have a good laugh at God's expense. Personally I'd like to thank you for showing us all, once again, who you truly are. And in regard to me defending God, well, He's big enough to take care of himself. He'll sort things out, eternally, in the end. So . . . if you're cool with mocking Christ, his sacrifice and his disciples, I'm cool with it too. Wasn't that easy? Proceed on.

Oh, by the way—for my fellow beer drinking buddies who are equally fed up with egregious attacks on traditional values—you can hammer these guys and their sponsors right in their wallets by not buying Miller beer, one of the sponsors of the Folsom Street Fair. I say, given their attack on Jesus that we officially never purchase another Miller beer ever again until Christ returns to kick butt and take names. Does that sound cool?

Chapter 3.

A Christian Can Be a Christian or a Liberal, but He Can't Be Both

—ɯ—

Can a Christian be a liberal? Short answer: no. There is no way a Christian can buy into neo-liberal ideology and be faithful to the bigger-than-Dallas teachings of Scripture and expect to continue enjoying his hard-won religious liberties.

For the "Christian" to lean politically to the left means that he must blow off huge chunks of the Bible and replace Scripture with the make-believe notions of postmodernism's malleable "Christ." Only after torturing Scripture can the Christian then fit liberalism into his supposed relationship with God.

For the Christian who believes that unfeigned faith in Christ should correspond with Jesus' high view of Scripture, it is impossible to believe in God and be an adherent to postmodern liberalism.

Liberalism has been hijacked by bizarre special-interest thugs who defy the Word of God and believe that the Bible has no place in public life (except maybe in a museum where people can look at it from time to time).

The Christian skipping around the maypole wearing his rose-colored glasses who has a bent to the liberal left needs to understand something: If it were left up to the modern, secularized liberal establishment, Christians would be more restricted than Bill when Hillary's in town. If the Christophobic thugs had it their way, Christians would be relegated to a marginalized spiritual ghetto on the sidelines of life.

For the naive Christian voter who thinks he can toss a ballot in the Nuevo liberal direction, please know that a vote toward the secular left could leave you bereft of sacred liberties. Thanks to the aggressive and ludicrous liberal lug nuts' anti-Christian agenda, your vote for a liberal Christian is a vote for:

1. Christianity to be scrubbed from government and whatever turf the government owns. Thanks to the liberals, the Ten Commandments have about as much acceptance in our government and their properties as Rush Limbaugh would at Harry Reid's family reunion. The Judeo-Christian principles that formed the rock-solid foundation of this great American Experiment are now aggressively and consistently attacked by the lascivious left.

If . . . if . . . the secularists continue to stay behind the wheel of this American bus, you can kiss all semblance of Christianity good-bye in this heretofore God-graced government. Saint, you might as well say farewell to our government's recognizing Christmas and adios to Good Friday if you're going to vote the liberal ticket. If the secularists have it their way, Easter will be behind your keister, and you can kiss the Cross good-night as an acceptable public symbol that represents your faith and our nation's recognition of Christ's atoning work.

2. Secularism to be continually mainlined into our public school system. Thanks to rabid, vapid secularism, our public schools and universities would rather you be a Rocky Horror super freak than a Christian. If your beliefs run to the bizarre or the banal or if you want to smoke the same philosophical

crack that Caligula, Nero, Castro or Lenin freebased, they'll accommodate you.

Our schools are totally open to anyone and to anything, unless, of course, you're a Christian. And if that's the case, then you're likely to get more sympathy from a badger with minimal sleep than you will from liberal educators who are hard at work making your life hard. Let me repeat: A vote for the secular left is a vote for Christianity to continue to be officially vilified on campus and for Christians to be ostracized in campus life.

3. Public officials, employees and appointees to be pressured to hide their faith in the closet and suppress their public displays of belief in God lest they be grouped with Hitler, Osama, or Mussolini and then fired. Not only will the liberals aggressively work to prohibit the State from green lighting and recognizing Christianity as a legitimate and positive force in our land, they will also attempt to stifle Christians from influencing the path of government.

4. Public attacks on churches and Christians and attempts to restrict them in the private sector. Consider this, Christian pastor and Christian lay person looking to vote for the ludicrous left: The secular Mafioso's intent is to make your ministerial life difficult, your evangelistic work taxing and your voice minimized. And good luck, pastor and church committee, in trying to buy property and get zoning with the anti-Christian libs at the helm.

5. The continued media endorsement of the same putrid, hedonistic stuff that sunk ancient civilizations. With the liberals in place, expect more weird crap in movies and on television. Expect to see more paintings of Christian symbols and saints smeared with elephant dung. Expect Christianity to be bashed and vilified and Christians made out to be buckled-shoed morons with three teeth and an IQ of 50. Expect the culture to coarsen. Expect your kids to continue to be exposed to things that only rock stars see backstage

with groupies. A vote for a liberal is a vote to see Christians continue to receive special ridicule and be flogged more than a piñata during a Cinco de Mayo festival.

Modern liberalism tosses out Scripture on several different levels. How a true believer in the Christ defined by Scripture can buy into what Jesus, the prophets and apostles said and also give credence to what these secular goons say is beyond me. In addition to liberalism's obvious and odious pro-Holocaust-like abortion stance, its anti-biblical view of marriage, its Scripture-slamming, aggressive secularism, and its feckless view of our nation's defense, liberalism completely clashes with the Christian worldview. Secular liberalism's aggressive desire to eradicate Christians' rights should cause Christians to be concerned.

The Democratic Party's liberalism has degenerated over the last 40-50 years in regard to its view of Christianity and Christian rights. This party, which formerly embraced and protected our nation's great Christian heritage and teachings no longer does so. Thus, today the Christian is between a rock and a hard place: He can either be a Christian or a liberal—but he cannot be both.

Chapter 4.

The Ten Commandments for My Daughter's Potential Boyfriends

—⚏—

God, in His providence, has seen fit to bestow upon my wife and me two beautiful girls whom we must steward into greatness. It has been a blast watching my daughters develop into righteous and rowdy, gorgeous girls. The thing that sucks with their metamorphosis into womanhood is the guys who've begun to buzz around our happy nest interested in my ladies.

As much as I don't like the idea of their dating, I have got to suck it up and accept it (bartender, I'll have a shot of whiskey). All you dads who are worth your salt and give a crap about your kids . . . you know how hard it is to let your girls go (I'll take another shot, please). Even though I'm slowly coming to grips with my kids growing up, I'm not throwing out my brain and becoming a hip and groovy dad who curls up in the corner in the fetal position without an opinion regarding their dating life.

Not only do I have an opinion regarding wannabe suitors, I have 10 commandments for potential boyfriends. Yes, seeing that I'm still the Alpha dog of the Giles castle, that I still pay the bills, buy the SUVs, pay for college and secure their condos, then by God, I'm still makin' the rules. I am Doug Almighty, got that Rico Suave? What I'm about to reveal unto you is an attitude-laden afflatus, so . . . be afraid. Herewith are my 10 commandments for my daughter's potential boyfriends. Read them and weep:

1. Thou shall understand that your presence doesn't make me happy. Young squire, don't expect me to be giggly when I meet you. As a matter of fact, you're ruining my life right now. Therefore, don't try to be cute with me. That stuff may work on my daughter or my wife, but it does not work with me.

Actually, you should expect nothing from me in the way of the warm and fuzzies. You've got to earn that. I don't care who you are or who your momma is. Your presence represents a transition that I'm not really ready for, so just stay the hell back and be real cool. And know this: I've got a PI doing a background check on you right now.

2. Thou had better have a life. My wife and I have worked our butts off providing a good life for our girls; therefore, you better have one, Spanky. Let me spell it out for you just in case you don't get it: You must have something positive going on in that thing you call a life.

Additionally, you must be pursuing said noble goal at Mach 2 with your hair on fire. If you're a slacking, blame-shifting, visionless slug with anal warts who's waiting for someone to carry him into greatness and lives by the dictates of his ding dong, then you need to find a girl who doesn't have a father like me.

3. Thou shall not touch my daughter, or I'll tear your hands off and you'll have to "whip the bishop" with a stub. Not only am I not cool with your being around me, I'm sure as heck not down with your touching my daughter. Therefore, when you're in my space (and in my absence) you'd better treat my daughters with the utmost respect.

Do not under any circumstance hang all over my daughter, fondle my daughter or soul kiss my kid until you have a wedding ring on her finger, a joint checking account and

The Ten Commandments for My Daughter's Potential Boyfriends

MMA at Wachovia—or I will shove your Justin Timberlake ass off my 3rd floor balcony first chance I get, capisce?

4. Thou shall look me in the eye, shake my hand like a man and turn off your cell phone. I don't care how Snoop Dog acts and what you've seen on MTV or in the movies. If you come into my house mumbling, with your shades on and texting the entire time you're around me, you're probably going to be spending the next couple of days in ICU.

I want eye contact. I want you to see my soul, son. I want to look you in the eye when I communicate things regarding my girls and their lives. So, take the shades off, Hollywood. In addition, if and when I extend my hand, grab it like you mean it. Where I come from, a limp handshake = a limp life, Twinkle Toes. Also, when you're at my casa, your phone goes on vibrate. I'm sure you'll like that.

5. Thou shall understand that you are a boy talking to a man. Here's some 411 to meditate upon before you address me. I am at least twice your age. I used to be a drug user/dealer until God zapped me. I've been in many fights. I've shot at felons. I faced down too-many-to-count charging wild boar. I've spent years in Tae Kwon Do. I've traveled the planet, planted churches and started businesses. You, on the other hand, use Proactiv and drive a Ford Focus; therefore, you will call me "Mr. Giles" and my wife "Mrs. Giles" until we tell you any different.

Also, don't gush around me nor attempt to read me an entry from your journal. I'm not Oprah or one of your metrosexual buddies that you can share all of your inner fears and deepest needs with. I am a Neanderthal.

6. Thou shall know that our family is old school. Do not even think about approaching me with liberal, hippy, agnostic, atheistic, anti-American or tree humping bull crap. I was raised by country-loving, God-fearing, hard-working, meat-eating, good ole' Texan parents, and I have zero tolerance for what your long-toothed, rather mannish lesbian

sociology teacher at Columbia U programmed you with—you dig?

7. Thou shall know that I like cool and expensive gifts, and you shall provide unto me this bounty—if you're smart. One great way to earn my favor is to buy it. Yes, you'd be shrewd to approach me like the three wise men did baby Jesus, namely with gold, frankincense and myrrh.

For example: I like high-quality cigars (nothing below a 90), Johnnie Walker Blue Label, Chimay Grand Reserve, books on hunting Africa and old British double rifles. I also like original artwork, R&B and classic rock compilations, collecting skulls, hunting and big game fishing trips, antique Christian and Classic books, custom choppers and early twentieth-century African safari memorabilia.

Who knows . . . I might, *might*, ask you to join me for a nice cigar session with me and the boys if thou comest bearing such offerings.

8. Thou shall understand that if you're dumb enough to tell me a dirty joke, I'm comfortable enough with kicking your butt. I'm not one of your thug buddies you can go down the gutter with. I want maturity when you are around my family.

9. Thou shall keep your word. If you say you're going to do something, then I expect you to do it. You see, I'm looking for stability/reliability for my ladies, and keeping your word in the smallest matters tells me that you're ahead of the pack and at least a consideration, in my mind, for our support.

10. Thou shall do these three things: 1) Look good. Do not come into my house with earrings, a grill, or oversized pants with your butt cleavage hanging out. 2) Read. If I have to talk to you, you had better know as much about as many things as possible. 3) Serve. I'm looking for a sacrificial dude who doesn't mind getting his hands dirty in helping

around the house, in our community, in our nation and in our wonderful world.

If you, young man, obey all the words written here, then and only then will you have a chance with my babies. Now, go get me a beer.

Chapter 5.

The Ten Commandments for Husbands

I hate to sound like some religious nut job here—but I really felt (sort of) for certain that God gave me, and me alone, the 10 Commandments for Husbands last Wednesday while I was watching American Idol.

"God inspired you to write this?" you say. Yep, God did. The way I'm almost certain it was maybe God speaking to me is that every time He speaks to me about something (and it's pretty often), I begin to smell WD40, packing popcorn begins to fall from the ceiling of my trailer house, and then a voice begins speaking to me in English—but with an angry and commanding high-pitched Chinese accent. It's quite an experience.

Given all these divine attestations, who can doubt that what I have penned for you husbands is anything but inspired? Stand in awe, all ye husbands, because herewith are 10 things that thou must doeth . . . or I guess *not* doeth—actually, there's both—to have a successful marriage.

1. Thou shalt not demand that thy middle-aged wife look like one of Hef's 20-year old chicks. Staying attractive for each other via exercise, diet and, possibly, a little nip/tuck, is one thing. Demanding that thy 45-year old wife look like a 19-year old Hillary Duff after she's received multitudinous stretch marks from giving birth to thy three kids puts thou

solidly in the running for the "Ass of the Universe" crown. Yea, such an attitude officially ticketh off the Lord thy God.

Palm Pilot, listen to the prophetic word, thou must be content with loving thy wife and appreciating her as an attractive and mature woman. She's not 20 anymore, and by the way, neither art thou (or is it thee?). As a matter of fact, thou probably art a paunch-gut sluggard with severe halitosis whose hair is both turning gray and loose. Thou shouldst be real thankful that she doesn't turn the plastic surgery/male enhancement gun on thou and thy . . . uh, shall we say, challenged areas.

2. Thou shalt not hang out with horndogs. Hanging out with guys who hateth their wives, who loveth to indulge in the superfluity of naughtiness and who are out to convert the faithful to the Cult of Infidelity is muy goofy. Be not deceived: Bad company will land thee in a strip club or an illicit affair which will causeth thou to meet with the chainsaw of Jehovah. Be afraid.

Husbands, if thou hast failed in the fidelity field, followeth these simple instructions: Own it, tell thy wife that thou art an idiot, beg her forgiveness, and goeth to counseling and have the sage tell thee what a bass ackwards brutish fellow of the baser sort you are. From there, go on, thou penitent one, to don thy frame with sackcloth, sit thyself on the front row of a goodly church and let God divinely redirect thy blood to thine big head so that thou can thinkest with that for a change. After that, pursue ye goodfellows who diggeth the whole married/family experience and let their light give thee light.

3. Thou shalt get a frickin' job. Thou sluggard, here's a little 411 regarding what thy wife is really thinking about thou not working: Your unemployed state is getting really, really, really, I'm talkin' really old. Sure it was okay for a fortnight. But after a year of thy lady bringing home the drachmas while thou surfest porn sites and watcheth Flavor

Flav—I'm sorry, I mean, as thou lookest for employment online . . . well, that's not cutting it anymore. Not only should thou get a job, but thou should be aggressively making certain that thou art constantly excelling at what thou doest and thereby, securing for thine homestead some serious flow. Hold on a sec . . . I'm smelling a fresh whiff of WD40. Yea, it's God instant messaging me . . . here it is: God IMed me just now to tell thee that thou needeth to roll out of bed, quit looking for a job out of thy window, feel the responsibility to feed thy family, be a big boy and do whatever it takes to provide for thy house—or get ready for Him to kick your butt (BTW: that was a direct quote).

4. Thou shalt lead thy family (Duh). Guess what, O man? You're to be king of your castle. I know, I know, metrosexual devilish misandry has taught thee to be thou a little princess; however, God would like, thou squeamish one, for thee to rise up and play the Spartan in the spiritual, physical and financial well-being of that which you betrothed and spawned.

Therefore, cease thou from shoving everything onto thy wife. Okay, thou passive twit? Learn how to manage thy money, get involved in thy teenage girl's life so she doesn't end up on a hip-hop video having beer poured down her cleavage while being called a "bitch and a ho" by a some punk thug who the hypocrites, Al Sharpton and Jesse Jackson, still won't condemn.

Get thou spiritually briefed and then establish for thine offspring a moral foundation that'll assist them to withstand the hedonistic hailstorm thy kid will face in . . . kindergarten. Pull thy head out of thy buttocks, shake the irresponsibility from thy soul, reject passivity and now go . . . lead your family courageously, thou formerly neutered Nancy boy.

5. Thou shalt not fart at the dinner table. Another thing that maketh thy woman want to trade thee in for something that runs on batteries, or for the young squire which cleanest thy cement pond, is to not treat her with R-E-S-P-E-C-T. Lo,

in all the places in which thee dwells and at all the times in which the Lord thy God allots your crippled butt to live, thou shalt show thy lady love.

This means that when thou sittest down to eat thou shalt not release thy fecal fumes. Unless of course, she does it first and bids thee to compete with her. Other than that, pinch it or excuse thyself to the land which is in back of the house in which thou liveth.

6. Thou shalt not speak down to her. Do not at any given time during the day in which God grants thee breath talkest thou to thy wife as if she is an ignorant and deaf dromedary. Yea, leave off being cruel if thou carest for the law of God, thy reproductive organs and if thou doesn't liketh thy coffee to strangely taste salty and if thou wishes to forego thy good lady lacing thy chocolate chip cookies with ExLax. Which leadeth me to the next decree.

7. Thou shalt cherish her. Thou shalt scrub from thy barely used brain the notion that tenderness is for wussies. Never taketh who she is and what she doeth for you and thy family for granted. Yea, the mother of thy offspring and the wife of thine youth is to be treated better than thy bass boat, West Coast Chopper and thy custom guns.

In addition, know this: The Lord thy God mandates that thou be courteous to thy mate, showing unto her gratitude and honor even when thou art so mad thou could spit.

8. Thou shalt give her time to chill. O man who likest to sit back, relax and scratch thyself, guesseth what? So doth thy woman. Therefore, relieve her of her duties and provide unto her the opportunity to do whatever the heck she wanteth to do. Thou diggest?

9. Thou shalt apologize when wrong, PDQ. If thou hast wronged thy wife, then thou shalt own it with sincerity and zeal. If not, the festering root of bitterness will develop and cleave thy union. In addition, thou mayest wake up with thy

skivvies super-glued unto thy privy parts for being thou the stubborn unrepentant jackass. Selah.

10. Thou shalt cut off communication with and never talk about your old girlfriends. Art thou so thick that thou needeth God to explain this one further unto thee?

Blessed is the man who obeyeth what has been written right here by this mediocre scribe. Woe unto the husband who thinketh that he can blow off the above and not feel the Lord's deep displeasure—not to mention that of the woman He fashioned. Amen.

Chapter 6.

How Wives Can Kill Their Marriage: Part One

"The wise woman builds her house, but the foolish tears it down with her own hands." - King Solomon (Proverbs 14.1)

If some of you ladies want to know how you can suck the life out of your marriage and drive your husband to insanity... or to the bar... or into the arms of another woman... or to a divorce attorney... or just shrivel him up into a conquered quail who inwardly loathes you as he dies a slow, emotionally torturous death, well then... this is your lucky day!

Here are 10 surefire principles that'll make your husband more miserable than Donald Trump being forced to watch Rosie O'Donnell River Dance naked.

They are...
1. Nag your husband.
2. Disparage him in public.
3. Keep him on a short leash.
4. Be a drama queen.
5. Hate his friends.
6. Hate his hobbies.
7. Cut him off sexually.

8. Get your parents and/or siblings involved in your marriage.
9. Never apologize.
10. Look bugly (butt ugly).

Are you psyched out, you masochistic mamas, that you are about to have at your disposal a demonic strategy to devastate your mate? You are? Then let's get straight to the husband crushing:
1. Nag your Husband. Nagging is an awesome instrument in the Torture Your Hubby Toolbox. For a wife to be effective at draining a husband's love for her and for life itself, she must not buy into this "loving, sweet, polite and patient" goofiness toward him.

On the contrary, she must be a nerve-grating, contentious, non-stop dripping faucet of fault-finding and finger pointing. Ladies, if you run out of things to nag your husband about, turn your spurn toward politics, church, culture, friends, neighbors, weather, work, or your children. It doesn't matter what you blather about—just blather. The point is to become a persistent source of audio pain in your husband's brain.

You'll know you've effectively wrecked his soul when he ceases to sing the song of your courtship, i.e., he goes from Clapton's "You Look Wonderful Tonight" to Elton John's hit, "The Bitch is Back."

2. Criticize your husband in public. Waling on your husband in private is good, but it is incomplete. What you've got to do, devil woman, is go the next step and publicly shame him. Melt him down when you're out on the town. If he's going bald, talk about it and how you don't like it. Does he have a little beer belly? Call him a pig and compare him to Brad Pitt. Did he have a financial setback? Tell your friends! Become a Tiger Woods at indiscriminately unveiling anything about your spouse that'll cause him to want to jump in front of a speeding bus.

How Wives Can Kill Their Marriage: Part One

Now, listen Broomhilda, you can humiliate your husband in many ways, such as the direct and deeply vicious, non-blinking verbal assault. However, the women I have witnessed destroy their spouses usually used humor. Think about it: Everyone will laugh (group derision is crazy effective) and you, the satanic wench, can say, "I was only joking." This will make him look weak (because he also can't take a joke), which will further blister the ebbing vestiges of virility he has left. This is beautiful . . . just beautiful. Try it tonight!

To be continued . . .

Chapter 7.

How Wives Can Kill Their Marriage: Part Two

From the negative reaction I've received from cranky women and toxic feminists, as well as the tremendous positive responses/confessions from honest and repentant ex- men emasculators, I think I'm onto something with my "How Wives Can Kill Their Marriage" series.

In regards to screeching female critics of my column, you and I both know that if I went to town on husbands (which I have many times . . . check my archives) everything would be cool. I would be loved and hailed by all the misandrists far and wide. Yes, the man haters would be giddy. However, when I turn my guns on the girls for their garish behavior toward their husbands, all of a sudden I'm a sexist, or a homo, or a . . . a . . . a something.

What's the matter? Can't take the heat? Listen, little Miss Can't Do Wrong, I'm here to tell you that, believe it or not, you're capable and oft times culpable for creating for your mate a living hell that is only surpassed by an eternal one.

For those women who want to become more efficient at eroding your husband's spirit, here are four more additional acrimonious assets that'll drive your hubby to drink massive volumes of alcohol and prefer angry leopard wrestling, listening to Yoko Ono yodel or Chinese water torture to your presence.

Having covered 1) Nag Your Husband and 2) Disparage Him in Public in my last column, I now offer you, the maneater, points three through six for your bitter arsenal.

3. Keep Him On a Short Leash. Third on my list for how you, the Satan woman, can kill your marriage is to place your husband on a short leash. Better yet, a choke chain. Your goal is three-fold: Make your man to feel, fear and heel to your wrath. You've got to verbally shackle him to your commands. Make him believe that he can't sit, stand, play, think, speak or spend money unless you, the queen condor, allow him to.

By short leashing your husband with an exacting set of laws, you will, in short order, morph in his head from being his lover to being his mother. This masochistic machination of insane restrictions will make your man feel like a stupid son, controlled by you, his new petulant mommy.

Forever gone will be the friend, fan, soul mate and confidant stuff that initially drew the two of you together. Once again, pure gold here, girls . . . pure gold. Listen, using this tip might not produce immediate devastating effects upon your man, but don't lose heart. It'll work, and he'll turn into a newt or move into the corner of your attic or joyfully leave you in the dust. Either way, this ditty will suck the wind right out of your marriage sails.

4. Become a Drama Queen. Another thing that'll make your husband long to be stranded in the Mojave Desert with no food or sun screen and only a rabid Rottweiler to keep him company is becoming a drama mama. Yes, your goal, ghoulfriend, is to ratchet up every situation so that you emotionally drain your man. Make the atmosphere of your home tense. Make everything, especially the small things, turn into a five alarm fire.

The thing drama queens do so effectively is jack up the stress levels in the relationship. This, naturally, robs the relationship of the fertile presence of peace. This redlining, high RPM spirit will stretch his nerves more out of shape than the elastic in Grosie O'Donnell's XXXXL panties.

Go for it, ladies. Sweat the small stuff. Yell, freak, faint. Sound the alarm, even if it's only over a broken dragon nail. If you concentrate you can make anything WWIII. Focus on wearing him out with your daily theater. Do not under any circumstance become a calm and well-modulated, peaceful and poised wife who can field any real or imagined problem that gets shot her way.

5. Hate his Friends. Separate your husband from his compadres quickly. You mustn't allow your husband to hang out with anyone but you. Sever those relational ties your companion has with those who have walked to hell and back with him because now, yes now . . . it's all about you.

You especially want to steer him clear of friends who feel the liberty and responsibility to shed light on you, the whacked wife. In addition, get your guy away from those buddies who have amazing and gracious wives or girlfriends. "Why?" you ask. Well, a loving, caring and an affirming couple will expose your broom riding proclivities and put needed pressure on you to dial freakin' down. Remember and beware: Trusted and wise friends are able to bring perspective to marital mayhem.

Therefore, slander his friends, vilify them and have stuff planned every night of the week 'til Jesus returns. If for some odd reason he steals a rare, uncontrolled moment where he and his friends can get a beer, try this: Just before he walks out of the door, start the washing machine, then cut the hose as the tub is filling and flood house. Or just set the drapes on fire. That'll keep him home.

6. Hate his hobby. Keeping the husband from his friends is not enough because your husband still has an out in his

hobby. Your goal is to joy steal anywhere pleasure can be had, and it is here that hobbies figure in greatly. Therefore, set your crosshairs immediately upon that which flicks his diversionary switch. You don't want him to enjoy anything that you don't like. Your duty: remove any recourse he has to find solace in something.

Additionally, hobbies create relationships built around shared likes, and remember, your goal is to keep him on a choke chain, with no compadres, sequestered in the house to listen to you moo. Never, under any circumstances, take an interest in his interests, encourage him in his pursuits and just simply let the boy play, as this understanding spirit could actually make him take a shinin' to you, and you wouldn't want that to happen.

I'll see you next week for the final four facts that'll help you fry your husband . . .

Chapter 8.

How Wives Can Kill Their Marriage: The Final Straw

I think the world is coming to an end. I didn't come to this conclusion simply because a lot of people actually read and like my column but primarily because of the tons of positive e-mails I'm getting from former livid ladies confessing their remorse for their previous acts of husband hating. It's crazy. It must be global warming causing all these ex-ice queens to melt and warm up to their men. See, global warming ain't all that bad, Al. Anyway, enough of the happy crap . . .

    I want to continue to feed the wives who want to snuff the life out of their marriage and make that thing more tedious that listening to Sanjaya sing "Riders on the Storm."

    Having covered "nag your husband and disparage him in public" in part one and "how to drive him nuts by short leashing him, becoming a drama queen, hating his friends and hating his hobbies" in part two, I now offer you (the bellicose beastesses of husband hatred) the final four fundamentals that will make your husband prefer being bitten on the crotch by a black mamba to your blah, blah, blah.

    7. Cut him off sexually. Another great way to make your man hit a depressed state that is only eclipsed by the one Rosie O'Donnell's proctologist deals with is to cut him off

from hot relations. I mean, give him nada. Guys will stomach some nagging, getting short leashed, multitudinous Naomi Campbellesque dramatic outbursts and your general disinterest of his interests—as long as you rock his world in the bedroom. Yes, most men are that easy.

Your job, Jezebel, is to ruin your marriage; therefore, it's not enough to rag and ridicule him and then run his friends off. No, you must go the second mile and turn into the Sex Nazi: "No sex for you!"

Yes, your goal, Cold Ethel, is to make Hillary Clinton look like Jenna Jameson. I'm talkin' about shutting the sex factory downnnnnnnnnnnnnnn. Cutting him off sexually will intensify his marital angst and could, if you're lucky, help push him over the temptation edge into an affair or into a crazy porn addiction or some other soul unraveling behavior like doubting his manhood, his sanity or his reasons for falling in love with you in the first place. Pretty cool, eh?

If you do ever have sex with your husband, you've got to make sure it's not out of love for him or the desire to have fun and enjoy his intimate company, but rather as the means to some sinister, manipulative end. Make your hubby sexually pay until he obeys. Here's what 'cha gotta do: When he locks step to your wishes (I mean to the "T"), then, and only then, do you dole out a little sexual treat. Get that whole Pavlov's dog thing going with him.

Under no circumstances should you show appreciation, be tender, fun, amorous and adventurous or do any other thing that'll keep the love flame lit. TLC, if injected into the marriage mix, will cause the two of you to have a healthy sexual relationship, which obviously helps a marriage (plus burns calories)—and that would completely derail your desires for marital misery.

8. Get your parents and/or siblings involved in your marriage. Forget this leave and cleave stuff the Bible dictates. If you want your union to unravel then you've got to gang

tackle your husband with la familia. For example: If you, as a couple, have a major decision to make, seek counsel and opinions only from your mom and dad, rather than your husband. This will give him that stooge/stepchild feeling of useless stupidity that is, FYI, a great alienating agent.

Also, does your husband need a job and does your dad own a business? What a great opportunity! Get your dad and his company to hire your husband. This will eventually require your husband to obey you at all times because now he owes his monetary butt to you and daddy.

Lastly, do not under any circumstances attempt to work out your marital problems between just you and your man. Rather, get your angry sisters, your lard ass brother and your mother who's nuttier than a squirrel turd to weigh in. Once conflict occurs, surround him in a scrum of familial disapproval. If not stopped, this clustering of belligerent kin against your husband will eventually do in the marriage. Since your goal is to tear down your own house, you probably need to call mama right now and complain about something your husband's done. If he hasn't done anything negative lately, just dig up something he did in the past. Or put a little twist on something he did with good intentions and make it seem like it was done on purpose to ruin your life.

9. Never apologize. If, in the odd event you do something that hurts your husband, or . . . say the unlikely occasion arises where you were woefully and ridiculously wrong on an issue, never, I mean never, under any circumstance, apologize for anything.

Why should you say you're sorry? You're the Queen of Mean, the Belle of Bitterness and culpable for nothing. You're not going to apologize because . . . uh . . . well, um . . . the wrong you did wasn't entirely your fault. Hello. He knows that. You have low blood sugar. And on that day when you screwed up and made yourself look like a donkey by wrongfully axe-grinding on your man, it was because you didn't have your afternoon Butterfinger fix. As a matter of fact, your husband, yes, your husband (whom you had put in charge of stockpiling your Butterfinger reserves) let the coffers run dry. Which means (that's right!) he is actually responsible for your demonic manifestation. Thus, it's him, I tell you . . . it's your husband who should apologize, dammit. You apologize? Please.

Whether it's low blood sugar, PMS, PBS, Global Warming, the vast ring wing conspiracy or Bill O'Reilly, you, the marital femme fatale, are fortunate to live in the 21st century. In this therapeutic age you are afforded excuses aplenty that will help you destroy your marriage by never owning or asking for forgiveness for your hellish behavior.

10. Look bugly (butt ugly). Women come in all shapes and sizes. The majority of men that I know (who love the testosterone, heterosexual, God-blessed fog in which they dwell) really like women. From Calista Flockhart to Queen Latifa, to them . . . it's all good. That is, as long as the ladies take care of what the good Lord has given them. The successful marriages I've seen know and abide by this golden nugget: Always look your best to constantly attract and show respect for your mate. It also aids in not terrifying dogs and small children.

Staying attractive messes with your husband's head. It makes him think, "holy guacamole" when he sees you. It makes him envision you while he's at work or out of town. It makes the boys' night out a little shorter—especially when you tell him, as he's leaving the house, that you've got the outfit from the lower right-hand corner of page 96 of the Victoria Secret's Spring catalogue waiting to be modeled for him if he's home by 10 pm.

However, since you're focused on mucking up your marriage, you've got to look bugly. Here's how it goes. Your husband's getting a little belly, so why shouldn't you match it? Or better yet, better it? You should blow off regular

How Wives Can Kill Their Marriage: The Final Straw

exercising, occasional tanning and wearing sexy perfumes. Don't bleach that hair on your lip, don't wash your greasy hair or follow current fashion; just plow on with your hellish couture . . . the oversized t-shirts, oily skin, stretch pants and that hair style you got from a 1906 Sears catalogue. To heck with your husband (and the world) if he doesn't like your looks. Your goal is to make him love you for who you are, not what you look like.

And with that, I'm done with "How Wives Can Ruin Their Marriage." Go for it, ladies. Maybe, just maybe, you can take Elsa Lancaster's old role in the upcoming Bride of Frankenstein remake. Work hard and keep your fingers crossed. Where there's a will, there's a way, eh? Don't deviate from these principles because if you do, you might end up with a happy marriage. Yecch.

One more thing: I've been asked by many people and talk show hosts if I'm going to do a series regarding how husbands can ruin their marriages. My answer: I'm not feeling it right now. There are plenty of books on Amazon.com that deal with that subject. And anyway, I think the boys have had their knuckles rapped for too long and for too much while the girls have been allowed to walk with impunity.

So . . . I wouldn't look for anything from me anytime soon on that topic. When things, blame wise, balance out—and if I'm still alive and if the price is right and I'm not hunting or painting or vacationing with my family . . . or watching grass grow or re-reading the operational manual of the hinge or having my fingernails slowly removed by an angry, sadistic midget with pliers—then and only then, I might write something which goes after the guys.

Chapter 9.

The South Sucks?

"Mississippi gets more than their fair share back in federal money, but who the hell wants to live in Mississippi?"
     -Charles Rangle, New York Congressman, 2006

If you listen to the Ditsy Chicks, if you like Rosie O'Donnell and if you think John Kerry is cool, then more than likely you assume the South sucks. Yep, our current culture has been brow beaten by the loons on the Left into viewing the South as societal swill.

In Hollywood, the hedonistic thought thugs make certain that Southerners are tarred and feathered as inbred, Ricky Bobby, moonshine slammin', KKKMart shoppin', fat back eatin', cousin humpin' square dancers with three teeth and an IQ of 50.

The liberal Belief Police want America to hate the South because the South represents the Secular Regressive's (SR) chief political and cultural (and armed, I might add) high hurdle.

The autoerotic "elite," which form the intellectually line-bred gene pool of the soulless Left, are hell bent to bar from our borders all praises and practices of the principles which have made the South substantial. What are the things that make Dixie so darn good? Well, I know it's hard for those of you who are wedged up Hollywood's backside to understand our virtues, but its stuff like author Clint Johnson points out in his predestined to be bestseller *The Politically Incorrect Guide to the South (and Why it Will Rise Again)* . . .

• A strong sense of patriotism that protects the rest of the nation. Dasypygals on the left who incessantly bash the South and hate everything sweet home Alabama stands for ought to eat a little sautéed crow tonight and send the South a thank you card in the morning, as the South makes up the overwhelming majority of the armed forces who protect our country and are willing to take a bullet for these ungrateful and derisive jackasses. The South accounts for 35% of the population, but 41% of the military recruits.

• A conscience about race relations. Johnson states, "The South has never denied its role in perpetuating slavery. The South and only the South have apologized profusely for its role in slavery." Since the slave days, "black income in the region has steadily increased, neighborhoods have been integrated, black politicians have been elected to major offices, and black business people have emerged to head national corporations. In the south regional patriotism trumps race any old day." And if the South hates blacks the way the way your lesbian US History teacher says they do, then why, according to the 2003 US Census Bureau, are hundreds of thousands of blacks blowing off the North and moving down South, huh?

• A sense of morals and religion. The fact that we haven't flushed God and Christ down the toilet, as the anti-Christ secularists want us to do, has made the liberal, tassel-shoed Nancys have a hissy. When other sectors of our society are shamefully caving to the godless cabal's secular agenda and keeping quiet about their convictions, the South sits back, yawns, scratches its belly, and then shoots these glib sisters a defiant rebel finger. In addition, no matter how much the liberal Presidential dopefuls play the "we like Jesus and

The South Sucks?

Moses, too" card in the upcoming '08 election, the South isn't fooled. We see the fecal fumes coming off their heads. Serious faith is a southern thang, a conservative thang, and not a 21st century liberal thang.

• A welcoming environment for business. WalMart (the world's largest retailer), Exxon, FedEx, Coca-Cola, Lowe's, Delta, Krispy Kreme, Toyota, Honda, Saturn, Nissan, BMW, Mercedes and Home Depot (as well as a slew of others) are finding that they don't need the Rust Belt to rake in the cash as the Bible Belt is working mighty fine for them.

• A creative atmosphere. Clint further prods the north by taunting them with their lack of creativity. He states that, "few folks think about 'northern literature,' but there is an abundance of southern literature. There's no such thing as northern music. I'm sorry, rap is a NY derivative. But then again rap is not music. There is, though, country music, southern rock, southern jazz, southern blues and bluegrass." CJ goes on to say that "there is something about southern lovers, rivers, dogs, ex-wives, ex-husbands, magnolias, pine trees, eccentrics, and soldiers that keep writers and musicians inspired."

• Real men. "Southern men are gentlemen, but they're also uncompromising, opinionated, and won't defer to what 'the group' wants..." America needs men who stick by their guns and southern men do just that. Southern men, saith Clint, don't flip flop; they stick to the convictions and principles they got from their families. Remember families?

• Real women. Unlike the female chauvinist pigs on the Left, Southern women are charming and ladylike, and like their menfolk, they have backbones of steel. Also, note to single guys: from Georgia peaches to Mississippi belles, there's no doubt about it: Southern women are prettier. Since the first Miss America pageant in 1921, one-third of the winners have been Southern.

In the latest installment of the bestselling Politically Incorrect Guide series, *The Politically Incorrect Guide to the South (and Why it Will Rise Again)*, author Clint Johnson exposes the controversial truth—the South is the essence of what's original, unique, and most loved about American culture. From the founding fathers to the frontier explorers, rock and roll to the movies, barbecue to sweet tea, NASCAR to NASA, slavery to segregation, no ugly rumor will be left standing in this book (from the press release).

"Today, there is an open, not-at-all-secret conspiracy to erase Dixie and all vestiges of the old South from public memory. The South is all about memory, heritage, and pride of place. I refuse to go along with the expunging of that memory, heritage, and pride. Only those things give us a true understanding of what it means to be a Southerner, and an American," says Johnson.

And here's a few more things that secular reality stylists don't want you to know about the South:

- Southerners wrote the Declaration of Independence, the Constitution, and Bill of Rights.
- The Civil War was not a true civil war, nor was it driven by slavery.
- Southern women had independence, equality, and freedom decades before suffrage.
- The South, not the West, started the Hollywood movie scene, blues, jazz, and rock and roll.

My advice to those who want to engage the secularists in the culture clash: Buy Johnson's book and get deprogrammed. What Clint has penned about the South is well researched, and it's funnier than a loud fart in church. You will not hear this stuff within the haggard halls of revisionist universities. More than likely, toward the middle of the book (if you love the US and how it was originally constituted) you'll start whistlin' Dixie, which was, by the way, one of Abe Lincoln's favorite songs.

Chapter 10.

I'm Not Homophobic; I'm Chick-O-Centric

I think I speak for most heterosexual males when I say I'm not homophobic but chick-o-centric. Let's keep it positive, okay? It's not that we dislike you, the gay guy; it's just that we really like girls. It seems no matter how long we compliantly spend in rehab undergoing the most stringent psychotherapy to rid ourselves of our knee-jerk to your mate choice, the simple fact is . . . heterosexual guys don't "get" gays. Period.

Heck, we don't understand women. What makes you think we'll ever understand a man who doesn't like women yet wants to be a woman? You just rifled right over our heads. In addition, not only are most men incapable of comprehending what a man sees in another man, we also don't care to try to because football is on—so can we all just shut the hell up with the gay stuff and watch the game?!?

Please, rehab freaks, you're wasting your time on the heterosexual tribe trying to get us to be cool with that which is incomprehensible to us. Just like the homosexual, we are quite happy with our sexual bent and our own little world, so leave us alone, por favor.

Now, this doesn't mean that heterosexuals hate you, the homosexual. It simply means we're focused on women;

which, by command, causes our paths of camaraderie to part. No, this is not a phobia, and it doesn't mean we loathe you; it's simply the funk of nature. As a matter of fact, I have several friends who are gay. I kind of view them like dolphins; they're fun, entertaining and creative. I truly enjoy their presence. I just don't know what they get out of eating mullet. My homosexual acquaintances view me in a similar light.

In the spirit of continuing diplomatic relations with homosexuals, you, the gay person, has to help me out a little bit. If girls are so icky and men are so mondo-jovial, why do you and a lot of your reps take on feminine mannerisms and dress? I would think that if you are going to be gay you would at least be a man about it.

It's the same thing with many lesbians. I don't get you. When I hear you speak, it's always "men suck, men are beasts, women rule," yet some of you "ladies" dress and act like men. You wear men's Dockers, men's Polos, you've got a short, man's hair cut, you're looking like Joe Pesci with breasts. You're an ugly version of us. I'm just thinking out loud here. What's-the-dillio? Please explain. It seems as if you would embrace femininity in all its glory like Carrot Top does red hair coloring. Where am I going wrong?

Now, let me help you, the gay constituency, to understand us girl lovers a tad. Most chick-o-centric males would not raise an unwaxed eyebrow at a homosexual man if he would not shove his gayness in our faces. It's the flamers that freak out most heterosexuals. Case in point: Bobby Trendy and Jay Alexander. They seem like nice guys, but the pink hair, lip gloss, heavy eye liner, constant limp wrist and lisp is overkill. Why not, instead of emulating a TBN host, you follow Rob Halford's lead? That would make it much easier for us to have a beer with you. C'mon . . . work with us, we're trying to get along.

Here are 10 more things you should know about most typical heterosexual males:

I'm Not Homophobic; I'm Chick-O-Centric

1. Just because we like art and fine furniture, wash our cars, regularly bathe and brush our teeth, and like nice clothes doesn't mean we're latent. What it means is that your team doesn't have a monopoly on taste or decorum.
2. No, we don't want highlights in our hair or a manicure/ pedicure.
3. We think Vespas are for beautiful girls to ride. Not guys. Harleys, custom West Coast Choppers, Triumphs, Indians or Von Dutchs = a dude's bike.
4. We don't like dogs that have "toy" as a prefix to their name.
5. A hunted wild animal's gut pile is a glorious and beautiful thing. Long live the hunt and the hunter.
6. Keep your lip gloss; we'll use our Carmex.
7. We like boots not flip flops.
8. Normal men do not like Celine Dion. If you see us crying during one of her shows, it's not because she struck a nerve with a ballad; but rather we are lamenting our manhood slowly draining away from us as we sit there, for the eighth time, and listen to this chick whine.
9. When we look at a pretty girl, we think "wow" and say, "howdy." To us, the lovely lady lumps trump a man's hairy back any day. Call us crazy.
10. We don't think Adam and Steve is an improvement or alternative to Adam and Eve. But that's just us.

The above 411 doesn't mean we be hatin'.

Now, lastly, for those of you heterosexuals who are in competitive sports and don't like to shower with gays, that's cool. It's your right to scrub your butt with whomever you choose. You gay guys should understand our reluctance and not make a big deal over it. I confess, I'm uncomfortable with showering with a homosexual, unless of course it was Portia de Rossi, and I wasn't married.

To remedy this situation, I propose the following: how about two shower facilities, one for the heterosexuals demarked by a gigantic poster of Beyonce's Sport's Illustrated Swimsuit cover and one for the homosexuals with a big honking 48 x 60" framed print of Ryan Seacrest wearing a chartreuse colored Speedo? There now... is everybody happy?

Chapter 11.

Anna Nicole Smith's Death Blamed on Global Warming

Our globe would probably cool off several degrees if Al Gore would just shut up and lose some weight. First things first, Al.

The unsubstantiated hot air that emits from Gore's pie hole, the friction heat his chunky thighs generate when he waddles, plus the greenhouse gas he bellows out his backside after scarfing down the grande enchilada platter at Casa Ole are enough to make a polar bear bust a sweat.

Speaking of polar bears, I do hope it gets a little warmer up north. I've always wanted to hunt polar bear, but it's just been too cold. Go warmer temps!

Back to Gore: You and I both know that Gore would be warning us about the negative effects of Spider Monkey urine if it would ingratiate him to the voting public. And that's what his god awful global warming warbling is all about: the unavoidable Presidential aspirations of Albert Gore. Jose Feliciano can see that.

Evidently, global warming didn't hit Texas last month when I was there during Dallas' Safari Club. It was cold. I'm talkin' Hillary chilly. Also, I believe it snowed in Malibu this year. But that, too, could be a sign. As a matter of fact, everything is now an omen that our orb is getting over-cooked:

- Lindsay Lohan's fire crotch? Global warming.
- Paula Abdul's speech slurs? Global warming.
- The tarpon bite has been a little slow and late this year in Miami?

Global warming. I've noticed also that the flying fish have shortened their glide paths. Coincidence? I don't think so.

- Anna Nicole Smith's untimely death? Global warming . . . or possibly, her opportunistic lawyer, Howard K. Stern?
- Astronauts doing wacky things with BB guns, love triangles and adult diapers? Must be global warming. Think about it.
- Could this also be the reason why Rosie's so angry all the time? The gradual roasting of our terra firma under her feet is making her irritated. Or maybe she's just plump and pouty. It's a coin toss on that one.

I was watching a guy on TV a few weeks ago talk about earthy balminess. He had his running helicopter parked on a slab of ice. As he spoke about our toasty planet, the viewing audience got hit with the obligatory sad seal pictures, melting snowman, gloomy Eskimo photos and a watery Slushy from 7-Eleven.

After his opening remarks, the snow prophet of doom pointed to a nearby ice bank and said, "Behold, even as I speaketh the ice melteth." I'm thinking, "Really? How about turning off the helicopter? The red hot engine and the 200mph wind storm the chopper is generating could possibly be culpable for your nippy apocalypse." I guarantee if he would have switched off Chopper 1 and held still for 30 minutes, Nostradamus would be doing his prophecy with snotcicles hanging off his nose and his hands crammed down his pants in an attempt to keep them warm.

As the earnest tree humpers try to convince us all that their moist Armageddon is a soon coming slip-n-slide reality, I'm kinda thinking that maybe, just maybe, they're full of crap, their stats are trumped, their science is specious, and this is a politically-driven liberal wet dream.

As a matter of fact, I'm sidin' with Dr. Richard Lindzen (Alfred P. Sloan Professor of Atmospheric Science prof at MIT) when he says, "Future generations will wonder in bemused amazement that the early twenty-first century's developed world went into hysterical panic over a globally averaged temperature increase of a few tenths of a degree and, on the basis of gross exaggerations of highly uncertain computer projections combined into implausible chains of inference, proceeded to contemplate a roll back of the industrial age."

In the *Politically Incorrect Guide to Global Warming and Environmentalism*, Christopher Horner shatters the global warming blather in 303 pages of earth cooling facts. He chills the left with several inconvenient truths for Al Snore, I mean Gore, and his 5 alarm cheerleaders. Stuff like:

- The earth has often been hotter than it is now.
- Only a tiny portion of greenhouse gases are manmade.
- Most of Antarctica is getting colder.
- The media only recently abandoned the "global cooling" scare.
- "Global warming" hasn't made hurricanes worse. Our tendency to put up trailer houses in their path is getting greater.
- There is no scientific consensus on global warming.
- Climate is always changing with or without man.
- Many big businesses lobby for global warming policies that will increase their profits—and our costs.

- The Medieval Warm Period was significantly warmer than temps today and was a golden age for agriculture, innovation and lifespan.

And these are just the tip of the re-freezing iceberg.

I'd love to see the alarmist, over-the-top doomsters of the left take on Horner's book page by page and try, with a straight face, to dismantle it. They couldn't do it.

God, if you are up there and you are listening to me and taking requests, I would love to watch a televised debate between Horner and Gore—or any one of his greenhouse gas sniffers. I'll even go so far as hosting it down here in Miami, Jesus. Please, Lord . . . will You make it happen? C'mon, God . . . I don't ask for much.

Amen.

Chapter 12.

The Teenage Casualties of Casual Sex

Chances are historically high, young person, that if you screw around sexually nowadays well, you could very well be . . . screwed. As in, for life, with the "gift" that keeps on giving—namely, a Sexually Transmitted Disease.

FYI young dudes and dudettes: No matter what they tell you on the various TV commercials, these diverse and multitudinous sex plagues aren't just a "little inconvenient" like a runny nose, halitosis or dandruff. They are devastating.

The entrance of an STD into your B-O-D could equal one or more of the following: perpetual physical pain, public humiliation, chronic depression, infertility, increased chance of birth defects in your kids (if you can still have them), cervix, penile and anal cancer and/or an early and horrible visit from the Grim Reaper.

Now, I know what most teenage crotch rockets and their aiding and abetting adult purveyors of the follow-your-little-head propaganda are thinking: "It could never happen to me. I'm special. That kind of stuff only happens to skanks like Courtney Love and Tommy Lee, and anyway, more than likely this is trumped-up parent/Bible Belt-inspired blather lathered up to make us keep our zippers in the upright and locked position."

The truth of the matter is that STDs are cranking in our culture like never before, and they are an equal opportunity infector. An estimated 19 million new cases occur each year with our teenage kids getting hammered with the lion's share of this slop (teens now make up 25% of the 19 million new "victims" annually).

Check out this smattering of factual 411 from Dr. Meg Meeker's new book *Your Kids at Risk: How Teen Sex Threatens Our Sons and Daughters*:

- This year, 8 to 10 million teens will contract an STD.
- Nearly one out of four sexually active teens is living with a sexually transmitted disease at this moment.
- Nearly 50% of African-American teenagers have genital herpes.
- Although teenagers make up just 10% of the population, they acquire 25% of all STDs.
- Herpes (specifically, herpes simplex virus type 2) has skyrocketed 500% in the past 20 years among white teenagers.
- One in five children over the age of 12 tests positive for herpes type 2.
- Nearly one out of ten teenage girls has chlamydia, and half of all new chlamydia cases are diagnosed in girls 15 to 19 years old.
- STDs accounted for 87% of all cases reported of the top ten most frequently reported diseases in the United States in 1995.
- This new epidemic is not just cursing those "poor inner city kids." No, the viruses have solidly taken up residence in the suburbs.

Yep, the reality is that every twenty-four hours 21,000 teens are slapped, saddled, infused and infected with some creepy, nasty and potentially deadly bug brought about by following the advice of our crass culture.

It seems as if following the guidance of the sexual revolutionaries of the '60s, American Pie, Superbad, Paris and Pam has brought about a veritable venereal tsunami of which our teens are now drowning in the disease-laden wake.

Imagine that.

Who'd a thunk that going indiscriminately nuts with your 'nads would end in anal warts, barrenness, a cauliflowered and inflamed penis, blown ovaries, ruined-for-life fallopian tubes, cervical cancer and a premature death? Wow. Who saw that comin'?

Y'know, I thought we could do whatever we wanted to sexually and the god of these goof balls, the latex condom, would save us all, baby. It's weird that with all the condoms in use today that STDs have not diminished but have rather skyrocketed. That's freaky. We all had so much hope in that $1.00 thin sheath of lambskin.

I guess the condom commandos didn't figure on new STDs showing up and ruining their party. Yes, the industrious little venereal buggers of the 21st century have found a way around the pesky rubber.

One polyurethane circumventor is the human papilloma virus (HPV). This dog is highly contagious and spreads via skin to skin contact as well as through secretions. Unless you get a HazMat suit you're at risk now if you're going to be a sexual player. Good luck.

For this pain-dealer there is no medication, no treatment that will eliminate this virus, and HPV is responsible for 99.7% of all cervical cancer and the deaths of 5,000 women each year. And most victims have no symptoms (just 1% develop genital warts) and no idea they have it until it solidly has them.

Young person ... let me ask you a blunt question: Is getting off with whomever/whenever worth getting offed by an STD? Can't you wait 'til you find some non disease-riddled person you love and stick with them? Is the need so intense that potentially dying for the big "O" is cool with you? If so, you need to dial down and get focused. Love yourself a tad more. Get a vision. Find God. Play Yahtzee or something because your obsession could come around and bite you in the butt, literally.

Here's my last word for the teenager: Nobody on the abstinence side of the sex spectrum is trying to keep you from having fun. We're just trying to keep you alive so that when you meet the right person and get married you can have a healthy sex life with no regrets, diseases, infertility or untimely death, that's all. And yes, it's come down to that. The sexual revolution is over, and we all lost. In this, your day, my young friend, there is a very real pay day for buying the BS our sex-obsessed culture is selling you. This is the hand you've been dealt. Be afraid.

And finally for mom and dad: Get Dr. Meg Meeker's new book *Your Kids at Risk: How Teen Sex Threatens Our Sons and Daughters*. This book is one of the most frightening and sobering books I've read lately. You will be chilled to the bone. If your GACF (Give a Crap Factor) is remotely engaged regarding your children then this book is a must-read. Be ready to be freaked out. Not only will Dr. Meeker sufficiently wake you up to the STD epidemic that is upon us, but she will simultaneously give you the wherewithal to help you help yours not be a part of the crotchal carnage.

One other thing—and don't tell anybody I told you to do this—but if you don't have anything to do this weekend, why don't you Google some STDs with your teen who might still be a little "iffy" about abstinence and check out the various photo galleries of the folks who followed the advice of our modern vice-meisters and played sexual roulette with their reproductive organs? It's scary. Very scary. You will all be gobsmacked. It's crude. It's rude. It's disgusting. But you know what... sometimes we need something that'll just wake us the hell up.

Chapter 13.

America's Obsession with Stupid Sluts

Have we, as a nation, become completely fascinated with stupid chicks—or what?!?

Girls, if you want to have our society's spotlight shine down on you for no real reason other than you're an idiotic, drunken, narcissistic whore, well then . . . this is your window of opportunity, girlfriend! (*Remember: the opportunity of a lifetime must be seized within the lifetime of the opportunity. You can get more successful loser principles from my new book, *10 Habits of Decidedly Defective People: The Successful Loser's Guide to Life*!)

Yes, ladies, if you . . .

1. are a semi-decent looking ditz with fake, cantaloupe sized ta-tas,
2. are a mediocre singer who can sort of dance at the same time,
3. are able to quasi-convincingly deliver a line when directed,
4. don't mind stripping once a Nelly song starts spinning,
5. are cool with having your crotch photographed more often than the Grand Canyon,
6. are okay with sleeping with various animate and inanimate objects while being filmed,

... then you need to get an agent because you have all the makings of star! I guarantee, Niña, you're about to become very rich and famous in this vapid and fetid postmodern milieu.

Americans, it seems, can't get enough of the immoral dumb chum that emits from the splooged brains like that of Lindsay, Britney, Paris and their wannabe ogling entourage. No wonder al Qaeda calls us the Great Satan.

For clarification purposes, lest someone think that I'm gay (not that there's anything wrong with that), I'm all for watching and appreciating beautiful women. But c'mon, America, enough is enough. I've seen these chicks' private parts via ET, TMZ and E! more than I have seen my own, and I'm 44 years old.

Y'know, it wouldn't be so bad to see these wacky wenches on our air waves if the media was fair and balanced in showing an equal chunk of accomplished women who have risen to notoriety without having to shine Clinton's apple. But that ain't gonna happen. At least not anytime soon. Maybe after the next terrorist attack on US soil wakes us the hell up. But not for now. As a culture, we have officially traded the applause we used to give to the truly noteworthy and have bestowed it upon the nebulous tramp.

You'd figure that after Anna Nicole Smith self destructed, died and went to an early heaven (cough) that these loose and loopy lassies would have learned a lesson. However, as Douglas Adams said, "Human beings, almost unique in having the ability to learn from the experience of others, are remarkable for their apparent disinclination to do so."

I can hear Paris' apologists now saying, "Oh, but these girls are cute, and what they're doing is just part of adolescent high jinks. After all, as Cyndi Lauper sang, girls just wanna have fun." Yeah, they're cute. And yes, it's entertaining. That is, until one of these oxygen thieves kills a kid in one of her drunken driving escapades. At that point, the cuteness and the amusement and our cavalier attitude regarding their asinine behavior will be officially over.

Chapter 14.

Anna Nicole Smithing

Not every girl wants an education, a righteous vocation, respect from decent people, excellent health, a happy family and the enjoyment of a long and fulfilling life. With the advent of Anna Nicole Smith and her ilk, Girls Gone Wild and Internet porn, it seems as if today's ladies would rather be known for no panties, making out with their girlfriends at Coyote Ugly, snot slinging drunkenness and having their college orgies broadcast on YouTube. You go, girl. Show you're right.

Get it right, you holier-than-thous: Not all lassies want a well-thought-of life. So back off. Some girls are chomping at the bit to step into Anna Nicole's bra and replace her as the next human freak show. And who are we to stop them?

Conservatives, and especially us Christians, should not judge people but rather help people fulfill their dreams—even if they are not our dreams. We must remember the 11th commandment of postmodernism, namely, "thou shalt not judge." Yes, within the secular would-be world, it is forbidden to forbid. Put that on you're refrigerator, you buckle-shoed killjoy.

So, instead of offering some legalistic and graceless judgmental blast toward those babes who are following (or wallowing) in Anna Nicole's path, here instead are eight helpful tips to assist you ladies in Anna Nicole Smithing (ANS) your way through life. Are you ready? You are? Then let's get busy!

    1. You've gotta have a "to hell with education" mindset. For all you ANSers out there, let me help you. All you need, as a maximum, is an 8th grade edumication. That's all. Barely finishing the 8th grade furnishes one with enough 411 to make retarded, irrevocable, life-demolishing decisions. So, just stop, drop and roll right there, girl. Anyway, everyone knows that 9th grade can be real yucky. With all that English blah, blah, blah . . . and the Algebra, crazy letter, math fraction whatever junk . . . and that PE stuff and the World Historizzle crap?!? Puh-leez. You don't need all that, girlfriend. Hel-lo . . .

    2. Wannabe ANSers, you must also blow off common sense and get married when you're 17 to the first 16-year old fry cook you meet. This little brain fart will get you the heck away from the house and all those people who rain on your dream of being the center of the universe.

    3. Next, to be an effective ANSer you've got to get an idol. I recommend choosing a deceased, drug abusing, divorced multiple times, lost soul known only for her looks, her promiscuity and her booze and dope dependency who died at a really young age as your god. Put her posters on your wall. Act like her. Have a plastic surgeon carve up your body to look like her. Then, go bonkers doing what you imagine she would do if she wouldn't have OD'd on Nembutal. In addition, sell your soul down the river and fully employ your faculties to become recognized as an equal (or a better) ditz to the dead chick you worship. You must have a vision.

    4. When earning minimum wage starts slapping you around, instead of getting an education, retooling and rethinking your multiple idiotic decisions, just start showing guys your boobies. You can begin wherever you are. You can make good money doing this. And we know life is all about

money, don't we? For instance, you can do this for cash in the break room at WalMart or next to the deep fryer at Krispy Fried Chicken (watch out for that hot grease, though!). Once you plow through decency and your conscience has decayed enough, I would then go public with your act. Look, your body is what God (if there is a God) gave you, so why shouldn't you trade off of it? I can't think of any reason why not to. A girl's gotta do what a girl's gotta do, right? Y'dam right.

5. When you, the ANSer, begin a life of stripping or some other form of pornography, the probability of becoming self-conscience about not having 36EEE puppies might start to wear on you. If you happen to be mammary challenged, you need to follow Anna Nicole Smith's lead and jam huge silicone sacks into your chest. On second thought, forget the silicone and stuff your chest with 15lb Everlast medicine balls. Kawabunga! That'll get you some Benjamins.

6. To move up the ANSing ladder you must give a lap dance to some billionaire Methuselah who looks like Gollum. I'm talkin' about a very, very wealthy and nutty octogenarian. Not only that, but you've got to bump and grind him so well that he coughs up not only his dentures and the Similac snack he had that afternoon, but a wedding ring and half a billion dollars. C'mon girl. Snap that thong, snap that thong, get a diamond ring and bang that gong!

7. Another thing that'll help you scoot on down the ANSing road is to turn your vagina and all other orifices into a revolving door. Yes, when you want something like a Louis Vuitton purse, a Toyota Camry, a Tiffany charm bracelet, a breast upgrade, lip injections, Methadone, the principle part in a D-grade lesbian sci-fi flick or a house in the Bahamas . . . well, the best way to get your way is to have sex with whoever has the denari (remember point 6!). Look, that's easier than all that working/waiting nonsense, isn't it?

8. If you, the ANSer, choose to procreate, just make sure you do not cease your selfish and hellish lifestyle and that your kids get swamped in your wake. First of all, if you want to have a child, instead of having your kid with one man that you love, I suggest having intercourse with several men in ages ranging from 20 to 70, from photographers to princes. Secondly, to make sure your mayhem has a multi-generational effect, drinking and doing drugs while pregnant is a good way to accomplish this end. Thirdly, as your child grows, let him see that you never abandoned your destructive habits. Fourthly, if your weirdness doesn't seem to be adversely pummeling your child, then surround yourself with creepy, opportunistic lawyers, folks with better drugs, TV producers who'll give you big money for staying wasted and "yes men" who'll never tell you that you are a stupid, stupid woman.

Remember ladies, when you're attempting to court catastrophe and don't know what to do, simply pause and ask yourself the question, "What would Anna Nicole Smith do?" Then follow suit (keeping the above list handy is helpful, too).

Look, Anna Nicole didn't live long, but she looked like she was having fun—didn't she? She was on TV a lot, which was pretty cool. Since we have evolved from the fairy tale stage of religious beliefs in all that personal accountability, salvation and damnation stuff, we can rest assured that Anna Nicole has simply passed (as you will also) from one party to the next. Therefore, proceed on, girlfriend, and keep on Anna Nicole Smithing!

Chapter 15.

Gun Free Zones:
A Mass Murderer's Wet Dream
(Written April 21st, 2007)

My heart is sick. I feel so sorry for those who were murdered at Virginia Tech, as well as the parents and loved ones of the slain students and professors—and all of us here at ClashRadio.com pray for those whose lives were just senselessly shattered.

But imagine if at least one Virginia Tech student (with a concealed weapons permit) had his .40 caliber Glock with him, locked and loaded, when this little Charlie Chan chump began his murderous mayhem last Monday on the Hokie campus? What would have happened differently? Would idiot boy have been able to slay 32 students and professors? I doubt it. But then again . . . who knows?

However, I'm a guessin' that this terminal turd might not have dealt out as much death (if any) if the good guy with the gun drew down on him and double-tapped the center mass of this ass with a couple of 165 grain COR-BON jacket hollow points. Yes, if there had been a good guy with a gun, who was licensed and allowed to carry it into class, he could have sent this spawn of Satan to hell where he belongs. In Hades, Cho could, forever in eternity, whine to Hitler and Beelzebub about rich kids, cognac, loneliness and hedonism while wearing a baby blue "Poor Frickin' Me" T-Shirt and pink tutu.

Unfortunately, there was no concealed weapon in the possession of a concerned citizen to stop this satanic weed from taking root because guns are disallowed on campus. Correct me if I'm wrong, but haven't the majority of the mass murders within the US in the last 20-30 years been in the Gun Free Zones? Why don't one of you industrious bloggers Google that stat and get back to me?

Gun Free Zones turn the people who inhabit such places into sitting ducks for insane whack jobs with death wishes. I know, I know, there are campus cops and security guards with plastic badges, golf carts, walkie talkies and pepper spray; however, as a soon-to-be father of a college student, that line of defense brings zero comfort to me if serious bullet flying $#*& starts hitting the fan in one of her classes.

Look, even the best Rambo-like police force equipped to the teeth, driving Vipers and descending en masse on campus in Black Hawk helicopters could not have responded fast enough to kill this Killer Korean Kid. But a fast thinking, well-trained student or professor could have.

I hate to seem pessimistic, but given this post-911 era and our current crappy culture, I don't see an atmospheric break in this violent weather pattern. I guarantee that even as I type and our nation weeps, there is, somewhere in the United States of Political Correctness, some Islamic Radical or some other disenfranchised dipstick making plans on how he can trump The Question Mark Kid's quota. Chilling.

Until we realize that a trained, licensed and armed civilian is a viable force against these murderous foes on campus, I suggest that both teachers and students learn to capture and kill a murderous puke with whatever is at hand.

As a matter of fact, until they lift this Gun Free Zone zaniness, if I were at a university, I'd pack my backpack or have on my person these things:

Gun Free Zones: A Mass Murderer's Wet Dream

1. A big—I'm talkin' huge—sturdy knife and fork. If anyone asks, I'd tell them it's for my lunch of Bumblebee Tuna.
2. A roll of quarters. I'd hold it in my fist and clock any SOB out to do us harm.
3. A rod iron walking cane made with a sharp handle. I'd learn how to swing it like Babe Ruth. I would practice smacking cantaloupes on the weekend.
4. A high voltage tazer. "High" being the operative word.
5. A seeing-eye pit bull. This wouldn't fit in the backpack, and I'd have to pretend like I was blind—but whatever it takes.
6. A letter opener that happens to be long enough to reach a lung.
7. A pet rock. I would officially adopt it and learn how to fling it like King David.
8. A black belt in martial arts. I'd start with Jiu-Jitsu.
9. A wrist rocket. I would just happen to have a dozen pinballs with me at all times.
10. A chair. This, too, is something I wouldn't need to carry around with me all the time. But since chairs are readily accessible in most university classrooms, I'd learn how to throw one with deadly—or at least diversionary—precision.

I know the above is not pretty or pleasant, but when foul devils can walk into a classroom and kill Amish school girls and innocent college students, as far as I'm concerned, the gloves have officially come off. My advice to students, professors and school administrators is to forego the pep rallies for a while and instead have a "Stomp the Next Perp Prep Rally." You've got to unite. Develop a strategy.

Call me simple. Call me a redneck. Call me whatever the heck you wanna call me—but until we allow credible and licensed, proven and protective profs and scholars to carry a weapon on campus, we will see this murderous madness occur again and again and again.

Long live the right to keep and bear arms.

Chapter 16.

Southern Fried Children

I'm ready to begin a Charlie Bronson vigilante campaign against teenage hoodlums who terrorize their families and our neighborhoods. How I would love to shatter the knee caps, prune the tongues and staple the lips of these demonic kids I see disrespecting their parents, elders and others with impunity.

With it being illegal to dust these little bastions of bad behavior (unless they commit a forcible felony against me) I've come up with an alternative avenue to release my angst, as most efforts to change these terrible teens are hopeless. Only by becoming the prison bride of a big guy in jail, catching an STD or via a Damascus Road experience will these Legion-possessed lemmings leave their path of doom.

Therefore, I've decided to turn to you, the new parent, and give you some guidance in rearing that fresh little bambino God has just blessed you with. Omit these foundational lessons, and your kid will probably try to stab you in your sleep for not getting him the new Nikes he asked for.

The principles I'm about to volley into your court are not new or original. They have been a part of the South and its heritage for many years, and their roots are biblical. Herewith is my ripped-off version of the recipe I got from

Clint Johnson (who got it from Emily Post, who got it from whomever) for Southern Fried Children.

1. Don't flaunt your advantages. The Southern Fried Child doesn't flaunt who they are, where they went to school or their net worth. Yeah, the bells and smells, the incense and nonsense afforded by certain advantages (earned or otherwise) don't mean Shiite to a Southerner if used as a fig leaf to veil one's lack of character and humility.

2. Everyone deserves respect until they demonstrate they don't deserve it. The Southern Fried Child believes that all men are created in the image of God and should be treated with respect until that person shows they don't deserve it (like Rosie does on a daily basis).

That means you don't slap, spit or drop the F-bomb on your parents, sonny boy. I asked Ted Nugent one time what he would do if one of his sons told him to F-off like Kelly and Jack Osborne regularly tell Ozzy and Sharon to do. Ted said, "I'd tear off their head and _____ down their throat."

It's amazing to watch 3, 5 and 15 year-old kids unleash their venom on their parents and others and then walk away smacking their gum. If my kids ever did that to me or their mom, their teeth would be lying on the ground. The Southern Fried Child respects parents, old people, teachers, police, peers and opponents—unless forced by said person to do otherwise.

3. Titles are important. The Southern Fried Child still calls their elders "sir" or "ma'am." I've got friends who have adult children with families of their own who make a very nice living, are close to my age and still call me "sir." When the Southern Fried Child addresses a man, it is always as "Mr. (last name)" and a woman as "Mrs." or "Miss (last name)" until they've been green lighted to use their first name or nickname.

4. Everyone else matters before you do. The Southern Fried Child is here to serve, not be served. They do weird

stuff like open the door for others. They don't rush an elevator knocking down granny to get on first. When they come into a situation they assess what others might need, not what they can get from people or places.

5. Be helpful. The Southern Fried Child sees a lady with a flat on her car and helps her. The other day I was out in front of a Publix Supermarket and watched a burglary in progress. The guy ran out of the store, cash in hand, with the clerk and security guards chasing him. It looked fun so I joined in the chase. The clerk and the guard ran out of juice, and I (along with a cop) got to tackle the dude and jam his face into the cement (one of those little perks God drops in your lap every now and then). Bottom line with those raised south of the Mason-Dixon is: Whether it's with tackling a punk or packing a trunk, The Southern Fried Child is programmed to H-E-L-P not hinder.

6. Be friendly. The Southern Fried Child smiles. They're not sullen or vexed. They're not walking around like the psycho chicks and metrosexual males in Miami in a pout pretending to be the next angry supermodel. The SFC says hello and starts friendly conversations. When I take my buddies hunting with me to Texas or Alabama, they're blown away at how friendly people are. We'll be driving down a Farm to Market Road in the middle of nowhere, meet a truck coming the opposite direction, and our host will wave. Invariably, one of my friends then asks, "Who was that?" and our host replies, "I don't know." Then my jaded friends give me a confused look and ask me quietly why he waved. I whisper back, "People down here are friendly . . . watch out—it might rub off on you."

7. Use the right words. When asked a question, the Southern Fried Child doesn't reply with "Huh?" "What?" or "Yeah." It's "Please," "Thank you" or "Yes or no thank you." They are kids who respectfully ask and don't demand.

Southern families, by and large, don't allow their kids to act like spoiled, rabid, egocentric animals. Good manners and propriety are expected of us "stupid" old rednecks and our offspring. New mom and dad, instill the above Southern qualities into your new baby, and when he or she grows up, they'll thank you in spades—and they'll be leaders wherever they go.

Chapter 17.

Let's Call God "Allah" and Jesus "Slappy White"
(Written August 18th, 2007)

Tiny Muskens, a Dutch Roman Catholic Bishop in Amsterdam, released another nifty idea this week upon his wooden shoe wearing sheep. Minister Muskens, well-known for stupidity aplenty, came up with a fresh game plan of which he said would aid the Dutch, yea, the entire world, in getting along with Muslims Gone Wild. Tiny proposed "that people of all faiths refer to God as Allah to foster understanding."

Well, isn't that special? How precious. God bless you, Tiny.

According to the Netherlands' biggest-selling newspaper, De Telegraaf, Tiny, after tabling his plan to reporters, said he had no further comment. He simply smiled, did a pirouette, stripped down to his pink boy shorts, put on a spaghetti-strapped yellow sun dress which he had in his exorcist kit and then started skipping down the cobblestone street with Boy George blaring from his iPod mini.

According to The Associated Press, Bishop Tiny Muskens (you can't make up this stuff, folks), from the southern diocese of Breda, told Dutch television on Monday that "God did not mind what He was named and that in

Indonesia (where Muskens spent eight years) priests used the word 'Allah' while celebrating Mass . . . Allah is a very beautiful word for God. Shouldn't we all say that from now on? We will name God 'Allah' . . . What does God care what we call Him? It is our problem."

I've got two problems with this priest's prescription:

1. The Catholic Church in Indonesia is not the pace car for Christian conduct. Hello . . . FYI to Tiny: of course Catholics in Indonesia are going to call God "Allah"—there are two of them and 234,693,997 Muslims. I'm guessin' that the Catholics over there are pissing their pants.

I bet they're feeling the same way I felt when I, the only white dude in a full theater, saw the movie Malcolm X the first day it was released. When asked by a rather large, pigment-blessed patron as the credits were rolling if I liked the film, I said, "of course I liked it. Whitey is the devil—and could you point me to the nearest well-lit exit?" Catholics in Indonesia do it? Please.

2. God doesn't mind what we call Him, eh? What god are you talking about, Tiny? Are you talking about the god of fearful and capitulating chunky Dutch priests? If so, I'm sure that such a squishy, imaginary, nutless diety that one's made up in his fetid and feckless fermented mind is completely cool with such a craven course of action.

Listen, Tiny, God's name/names are significant. Remember the "hallowed be Thy name" stuff the real Jesus taught in the Bible? I assume you had to at least scan Scripture at one time before you got that collar and started going around saying such stupid things in public. Listen, Father Feelgood, do a little word search regarding God's name and see if He cares what you call Him before you queue up with your craziness.

You will quickly find in this little exercise that God's name(s) denote His nature, His character, His person and His work. Much like yours, Señor Muskens. Let's break down your name: Tiny Muskens. Tiny, meaning very small, minute and wee. And Muskens, derived from the root word "musk," meaning a smelly greasy secretion, as well as an artificial imitation of the substance.

Why stop with just a simple name change, Tiny? Let's remodel everything we do to suit radical Muslims. I mean, we don't want to upset them now, do we?

To foster peace and Rodney Kingishness (can't we all get along?) we could do things such as . . .

1. Start calling our churches mosques.
2. We could call Jesus "Slappy White" because Slappy was a beautiful person, a great jazz guitarist—and he made some tasty BBQ ribs.
3. Yank the steeples off the roofs or our churches and replace them with gold domes.
4. Start circumcising our young girls.
5. Start killing homosexuals, adulterers and thieves.
6. Start oppressing women.
7. Fling open our borders.
8. Disband the TSA, NSA, FBI and CIA.
9. Start hating Israel.
10. Start hating America.
11. Grow long beards.
12. Scrap Christmas for a Mohammed's Birthday Blow Out Bonanza.
13. Replace Easter with Ramadan.
14. Bring on the burkhas.
15. Become liberals. And . . .
16. We could all start wearing Tiny Muskens' new Butt Kisser Lip Balm.

Chapter 18.

Christianity Sucks and Islam is Awesome?

Man, don't cha love how mainstream media and their soft-brain disciples make Christians out to be fish-stickered, bug-eyed equals to incensed Islam? If you were to accept as true what some atheists, secularists and prattling gay activists say about Christians, you'd think the church is chomping at the bit to chop off some heads of unbelievers, glory to Gawd!

Yep, if you were to believe the barf belched out by the BS brokers on the Left, you'd stagger away Kool Aid drunk with the belief that there is little disparity between conservative Christians and militant Muslims.

As a matter of fact, you probably would be bamboozled into believing that Islam is a peaceful, Little House on the Prairie religion being temporarily hijacked by jihadist renegades, and Christianity . . . Christianity is the real charity-vacant, vicious cult that's vying for the opportunity to seize the whip and whip us good.

Yes, the postmodern reality stylists are working their butts off trying to convince us TV-addled cattle of two primary things: 1) violent jihad is not based on the Koran and 2) All conservative Christians are theocrats ready to burn Sully Erna at the stake, stone Jay Alexander in a nearby gravel pit, and governmentally ramrod Christianity down everyone's pie hole.

I haven't seen this kind of ham-fisted, forced PR, farcical façade being parlayed upon the public since Michael Jackson tried to make out with Lisa Marie in an attempt to convince us all he'd found true love in an adult of the opposite sex.

Look, there's no denying violent things have been done by the church and in the name of God, but that has been the exception and not the rule. In addition, when the church has spent time with its head up its butt doing bogus things, the church's leaders have historically owned it when wrong, have not repeated the gaff, have grabbed the wheel and have effectively steered saints out of any erroneous, detrimental ditch.

Not so with Islam.

In Robert Spencer's new book, *Religion of Peace? Why Christianity Is and Islam Isn't*, Bob shows those who can still be shown anything factual the massive and fundamental differences between Islam and Christianity. They are not equal no matter how much the blah blah blatherers of political correctness purport them to be. Their beliefs are not similar, nor their practices, nor their means to spreading their message—and to think otherwise, postmodern Pollyanna, could cost you your rear.

Spencer points out the crystal clear facts that clash with the current anti-Christian hype such as:

- Most Muslims do not condemn jihad.
- Christianity and Islam have neither similar traditions nor similar modern realities—Christian religious violence, real or imagined, does not mitigate the reality of jihad.
- A "Christian theocracy" in America is a figment of the Left's imagination.
- The Islamic world has never developed the distinction between religious and secular law that is inherent in Christianity.

- Christianity has embraced reason—and Islam has always rejected it.
- The Koran does not invite interpretation, and Muslim leaders refuse to discuss how to fit their beliefs into modern society.
- Political differences and unwanted international interference are not, in fact, the cause of the turmoil in Iraq and Middle Eastern antagonism toward the West.
- Jews, Christians and peoples of other faiths (or no faiths) are equally at risk from militant Islam.
- The most determined enemies of western civilization may not be the jihadists at all but the leftists who fear their churchgoing neighbors more than Islamic terrorists.

Listen, 21st century truth reconstructors . . . you've gotta relax. Please do us all a favor and go get healed from your bad Sunday school experience and lay down your church grinding axe. Thinking people aren't buying the "Christianity = Islam" smack.

Get real, Goofy. You and I both know that regardless of what a few loopy CINOs (Christians in Name Only) have done via violence in the name of the Father that it is not in the body of Christian doctrine to hack off the noggin of the obstreperous. There's not even an obscure passage in the Book of Revelation that some demented clod could twist like your Gumby doll to make the Christian Scripture green light your demise or anyone else's. Additionally, Christians aren't longing for TBN to replace DC as our nation's headquarters.

So chill, you shrill shredders of Christianity.

On the flip side, it is within the pages of the Koran to convert, conquer or kill non-Islamic people. And I'm a thinkin' that no matter how much you work to besmirch

Christianity and misinform on behalf of militant Islam that if they had it their way, you, the secularist, would be a deceased grease stain on God's green earth.

Therefore, gay guy, loosen that neckerchief and relax on the anti-Christian rhetoric, okay? Atheists, dial down and go back to studying monkeys (or whatever you do), and secularists, switch to decaf and exhale because you guys are barking up the wrong tree in trying to paint Christians as a coercive, could-be-violent, cabal-like, militant Islam.

Radical Muslims, on the other hand, are the ones you need to sweat because their book has zero tolerance for the likes of Sully and Jay—or anyone for that matter who doesn't lock step. You can bet your backside that if uncut Islam were in charge, Christopher Hitchens would be history, Drew Barrymore would be nevermore and Andrew Sullivan would never be seen again.

The Judeo-Christian worldview (and subsequently, the great western traditions it undergirds) is the only powerful cudgel in existence to ward off militant Islam. That's what makes the Left's lies about Christ's Church and the Left's desires to diminish it so diabolical. If the church's presence and power gets marginalized via these secularists's anti-Christian propaganda, then all I've got to say is, "I hope everyone is cool with wearing burkhas."

Chapter 19.

Atheists Better Pray to God They're Right

Paul (not the lead singer of the Beatles, but the apostle Paul) states that God has made Himself known, via creation, to all men. According to the apostle, God's revealed Himself not just to Christians and to Jews, but to everyone everywhere (see Romans 1:18-21).

This means that from Jo-Jo the Brazilian monkey boy, to the Cameroon pygmies, to the whiny lesbian agnostic smoking clove cigarettes at Starbucks, to the beer swillin' dillweeds (what's up, dudes? I'll see you after I pen this column! Keep 'em cold), to the brooding British atheists, all people know God exists—even if they can't really put a finger on some of the finer points of His person.

Yes, through what has been made, God has plastered on the souls of earth's citizenry the general revelation that He's present. In addition, they also know when they're being a jack ass and when they're being cool (more on that next week).

I know the above 411 hurts the atheists to hear, seeing that they've staked so much of their imago on God's non-existence. But c'mon, you know there's Someone "out there," so cut the crap, shave your goatee and find some other way to pick up chicks—okay, James Dean?

Look, if Paul's right and people know that they know Him (even if it's in some dull sense of the word), why do some trip over themselves and tie their brains in knots in order to curb this knowledge? Why do people go nuts looking for loopholes and supposed contradictions in Scripture, hypocrisies within the church and some shared semblance to an ape in order to convince themselves that God's not here, there or anywhere and never has been nor ever will be?

Is it because . . .

They are Johnny Quest truth seekers looking to answer man's $64,000 question?

They are evolutionary luminaries uncommonly endowed with more smarts than us poor cattle and are here to help us club foot our way up the Darwinian ladder and away from such primal fairy tales? Or is it simply because . . .

The existence of God, His standards and a day of personal accountability really, really jacks with their efforts at autonomy and their chances of getting laid tonight?

The apostle Paul states it's the latter.

Atheists, according to Santo Pablo, have suppressed the truth because God really cramps their style. It's hard to persistently indulge the appetites of the flesh if there is a holy God to whom you must give account. The truth is that all men who have not bowed their knee to God and His way hate Him and are intrinsically geared against God (I know that's tight, but it's right).

Jesus put it forcefully up fallen humanity's tailpipe when He exposed why men reject the knowledge of God when He said, "Men love darkness rather than light because their deeds are evil. For everyone who does evils hates the light, and does not come to the light, lest his deeds should be exposed" (Jn. 3.19-20).

This is easy math, folks: A man who has no remorse and thus no desire to repent from his sins is probably not going to be a big advocate for the existence, person and work of God.

You know that all the various no-God arguments—which, to be sure, are fun to debate and write about and blah, blah, blah—actually stem from the root of the atheist's refusal to curtsy to what he already internally knows is true. It is this denial and refusal to embrace the general knowledge of God given through creation that officially pisseth off the Lord thy God and puts the atheist in a precarious position. My advice to my atheist buddies is this: You'd better pray to God that you're right and that He doesn't exist—because if you're wrong, eternity is going to be rough.

To be continued . . .

Chapter 20.

Hey Atheists . . . Get Your Own Moral Code!

I received a lot emails from snippy atheists after my column, "Atheists Had Better Pray to God They're Right," ran the week of May 13, 2007. I had many God-deniers tell me, quite self-righteously I might add, that they lived by a high moral code without the aid of any "opiate" or "crutch" like Jesus or Moses, and they didn't need some archaic holy book giving them the skinny on how they should live.

Hey, arrogant atheists, here's an aside before I take you to task any further: That self-righteous, "I'm good enough without God" attitude is the very sin that Christ condemned the most. But I wouldn't worry about that since Jesus probably never existed anyway. And if He did, He wasn't "the One" He thought He was and said He was and thus, all He said was a load of hooey. That is, according to your wizards.

Anyway, back to my point. Did I make a point yet? Please forgive me. My coffee is wearing off. Okay, now I'm tracking . . .

In the volley of hate e-mail hailed down upon me, one particular anti-God guy stated that he lived better than most Christians. He further patted himself on the back by saying that his Christian buddies even gave him big props for his squeaky-cleanness. Well, let me join in your hombres' praise by saying a big "good for you, dude. Here's a brownie button." I'll be the first to admit that I'll take a civil atheist over an irrational and violent al Qaeda op any old day.

The problem I have, however, with the atheists and their goodness and their morality claims is that all your ethical codes of conduct sound strangely similar to the principles inherent to the Judeo-Christian traditions. As a matter of fact, it seems as if you have bellied up to the Bible and are treating it like a buffet . . . passing up on the worship of the person and work of God while taking second helpings of His moral principles, you duplicitous little evolved monkey, you.

One of my old seminary profs used to say that although such muddled atheists would never verbally affirm the existence of God, they would live according to some ethical standard, some moral capital they have milked from us theists.

If I were an atheist and believed that God didn't exist, that the Bible was a bunch of weird bunk written by religiously deluded men several thousand years ago, that Jesus was an apocalyptic, sandal-wearing, hippie forerunner of David Koresh who went around spitting out cheeky clichés who needed not to be heeded but straight-jacketed or at least ignored—I sure as heck wouldn't be borrowing any tidbits of His wisdom to navigate my life's glide path.

If Moses, Elijah, Abraham, David, Jeremiah, Paul and Peter were not who they claimed to be and spoke not for Whom they claimed to speak, then these dudes were certifiably psycho and you wouldn't find me (if I were an atheist) taking any of their moral maxims and making them into inspirational refrigerator magnets.

That's what I appreciate about the atheist and philosopher Friedrich Nietzsche (1844-1900). Freddy is one of the few atheists who told his fellow atheistic buddies that they couldn't have their cake and eat it, too. Nietzsche understood that we can either have God and meaningful morality, or we can have no God and thus, all life is meaningless and without any trace of hope . . . it officially sucks.

Nietzsche came to the conclusion that if there is no God—or God is dead, as he put it—then he's not going to live "as if" God is alive and His moral principles mattered. Yes, brass-balled Friedrich said that the opposite of how the Bible says to live is the way we should live.

Nietzsche, unlike you postmodern Nancy atheists, was welded to his belief that God was dead and Christian morality was gonzo. He was not a half-hearted atheist parading around like most atheists do today, claiming the title while schlepping to Judeo-Christian principles.

Once again, if I did not believe in God and believed that the 10 commandments were BS and that faith, hope and love were for "the herd" and that I came from nothing and am going to nothing and there is no ultimate eternal accountability for my actions—then I am sure not going to live like I did. Why do you do so, Mr. and Mrs. Atheist?

So what's it going to be, my obstreperous amigos? Are you going to continue to blather on about there being no God and then live like there is one and that His word and will matter? Get consistent, why don't 'cha? Don't live by the Ten Commandments. Don't live by the Golden Rule. Don't do unto others as you would have them do unto you. That's our stuff. That's the Judeo-Christian way. Get your own commandments that are logically deduced from the "no God" hypothesis, write your own unholy book and form your own civilization. Then let's see how appealing it is, how it betters the planet and how far you'll get.

Chapter 21.

Why God Needs the Atheists

I get two things out of the nihilistic existence of the atheists: 1) astonishment and 2) a more rational faith. I'd like to thank you, my anti-God buddies, for both.

From an astonishment standpoint, I gotta hand it to you guys . . . you have huge cojones! Think about it, Christian: These folks are taking on God, bashing the Bible and slapping the church with only a 50/50 chance that they're either right or eternally screwed—and yet, they still plow forward with their faith in no faith.

What incredible, though non-religious, belief and zeal these God-deniers possess! You should bow and kiss their rings, all you Christians who are afraid to stand up for your convictions.

Say what you will, saint, but you must give the atheists major props for their steely nerve. Heck, most Christians won't say anything about Rosie, radical Islam, ecclesiastical heresies and hypocrisies or the licentious secular progressive agenda—but these dudes have no problem at all flying the finger at Jehovah.

We could use some of their brazenness in standing for what we "believe," don't 'cha think, Pastor Zero Nuts? Yes, in the daring department, I salute the atheist. Not only do the atheists hold me gobsmacked for their courage in light of a . . . shall we say . . . gloomy eternity (even if they're a bubble off level in their beliefs), but they also embolden me to be more serious about my knowledge of God, the world He created, humankind and Scripture.

Indeed, their full-throttle defiance of the Creator helps me to shore up aspects of my Christianity that are illogical, insipid and inconsistent. Again, muchas gracias, Jesus-haters, for keeping me on my toes.

Admit it, Church. If it weren't for the atheists busting our chops on a regular basis and asking us all the wrong questions, we'd be dumber than a bag of hammers, more duplicitous than OJ before Ito, and ickier than Johan van der Sloot. The reason being? Well, we don't church the church any longer. Generally speaking, you and I don't get that kind of intellectual challenge and intense rebuke within our entertainment churches.

C'mon Christian, you and I both know that most pastors can't challenge a congregant to quit being a stupid, hypocritical loser because that might cost him his crowd and the all-important tithe and offering—and we can't have that now, can we?

Face it, feeble faith holders, we have created in the American church an insular and gooey, hot-tub religion of feelings... nothing more than feelings... that non-religious thinking people despise. Subsequently, most nice Christians can't answer an earnest question from a third grader concerning the basics of their faith, much less field some of the serious smack a provocative Hitchens would throw their way.

This inability to give a rational answer to those who ask you why you believe what you believe is both a shame and a sin. It's a shame in that your ignorance makes you look goofy and lazy, and it's a sin in that it is in direct disobedience to the command to love God with all of your mind. Remember that scripture? You don't? Don't worry about it,

God loves you anyway. Hey, did you get your tickets to see Carmen at Disneyland this weekend? Yeehaw!

I know some of you are going to think I have wandered off the reservation, but I get more out of listening to Christopher Hitchens than I do Creflo Dollar. I profit more from watching CNN than TBN. Bill Maher benefits me more than Benny Hinn. How? Well, these men and their provocative questions, egregious and oft times erroneous assaults and merciless diatribes drive me to take stock of what I supposedly believe and what I do as a believer.

Where the church is insane, inane, lame and tame, you can bet your backside the atheist will be there to point it out. As the church, we cannot blow off this rebuke just because it wasn't served with a smile and a mint on a pillow. Correction, that's correct—no matter who delivers it—will do the wise good.

So, my brethren, let the atheists rage, let them ask their old and already-been-answered questions, let them tie your mind in a temporary knot and let them point out where we—the church—are goofy.

If you properly react to the atheists' scat, you'll end up with a more solid grasp on your faith, the incense and nonsense will be scrubbed from your life, and you just might dust them in a debate next time they queue up with their tired quips.

This is why God needs the atheists: to help the Christian not waver in his profession of faith.

One more thing: If you need some summer beach reading to help you run circles around the anti-God crowd 'til you take the big dirt nap, get R.C. Sproul's book, *Defending Your Faith: An Introduction to Apologetics.*

Chapter 22.

How to Shut Up an Atheist if You Must

The atheist's days of running circles around the Christian with their darling questions are drawing to a close. Yes, the fat lady just wrenched herself off her humongous backside, has cleared her throat and now is fixin' to sing the finale on the atheist's ability to have fun with their specious little fairy tales at the Christians' expense.

That is if the Christian will buy, devour, commit to memory and stand up and challenge the pouty anti-God cabal with the atheist-slaying facts found in two new books from Regnery namely, What's So Great about Christianity and The Politically Incorrect Guide to the Bible.

Authors Dinesh D'Souza and Robert Hutchinson skillfully answer, once again, the atheist's pet questions about the existence (or non-existence) of God and how Christianity has allegedly made the world suck. Suck, for you thick atheists, is a slang word which means to make or to be really, really crappy (kind of like how our culture becomes anytime you guys mess with it).

These books will be especially beneficial for high school and college students to draw upon when their secular anti-God fuming delirious instructors start railing against God and Christianity.

For instance:

1. When the prissy anti-Christs tell you the Bible stands in the way of science, inform them that the greatest scientific geniuses in history were devout Christians—and scientists from Newton to Einstein insisted that biblical religion provided the key ideas from which experimental science could develop.

2. When the pissy God haters tell you the Bible condones slavery, you can remind them that slavery was abolished only when devout Christians, inspired by the Bible, launched a campaign in the early 1800s to abolish the slave trade.

3. When the screechin' teachers tell you the Bible has been proven false by archaeology, hark back and show them that each year a new archaeological discovery substantiates the existence of people, places and events we once knew solely from biblical sources, including the discovery of the Moabite stone in 1868, which mentions numerous places in the Bible, and the discovery of an inscription in 1961 that proves the existence of the biblical figure Pontius Pilate, just to name a few.

4. When they get sweaty and tell you that the Bible breeds intolerance, refresh their memory with the fact that only those societies influenced by biblical teachings (in North and South America, Europe, and Australia) today guarantee freedom of speech and religion. Period.

5. When one of them queues up and quips that the Bible opposes freedom, smack 'em with the fact that the Bible's insistence that no one is above the law and all must answer to divine justice led to theories of universal human rights and…uh…limited government.

6. When they tell you that Christianity and the Bible justify war and genocide, unsympathetically remind them that societies which rejected biblical morality in favor of a more "rational" and "scientific" approach to politics murdered millions upon millions more than the Crusades or the Inquisition ever did. Hello. "Atheist regimes have caused

the greatest mass murders in history," says D'Souza. Inside D'Souza's book you'll find little gems like, "The Crusades, the Inquisition, the Galileo affair, and witch hunts together make up less than 1% of the murders that have occurred during modern atheist regimes like Stalin, Hitler, and Mao."

This is just a smattering of the various 411 fun the Christian is going to get as they plow through What's So Great about Christianity and The Politically Incorrect Guide to the Bible.

Senior pastor, college pastor and youth pastor: do yourself and your congregants a favor and teach this stuff to your church. Equip Christians to stand against the BS (belief system) of the atheists. The culture war is heating up, therefore make sure your people don't stand intellectually naked and neutered before these no-God numb nuts.

Lastly, comfortable and cocky atheists, you had better brace yourselves. Hundreds of thousands of Christians and authors are about to read these books and, as stated, systematically dismember your old and haggard arguments.

In addition, everywhere I go and speak—be it in conferences, on the radio, on television or in print—I'm going to encourage the tens of thousands of Christians I address that every time and everywhere they get crapped on by an atheist with unfounded arguments to open their mouths and slam dance them with facts found in these two new brilliant books from Regnery.

Chapter 23.

Atheism: An Intellectual Revolt or Pelvic Rebellion?

Atheists would love for everyone to believe that their motive for not believing is an intellectual one. Yes, the atheists ardently suppose that they are wise and the Christians, well, we're the buckle-shoed buttheads.

Yes, darling, the atheists would love all of us to suppose that they cannot believe because they are so astute and rational, and we theists, heck we're toads . . . a veritable troop of abecedarian simpletons who believe in God and Christ simply because we're straight goofy.

I think the atheists believe in not believing, however, not because they're intellectual little dandies but because they want to be autonomous, loose and randy.

As Dinesh D'Souza said about the atheist's faith in no faith in his new book *What's So Great About Christianity*: "Atheism is not primarily an intellectual revolt, it's a moral one." God, that's got to hurt you guys because you pride yourself on being so wise . . . so sophisticated . . . and here he/we are saying that your atheism rises out of hedonism instead of intellectualism. Ouch. Need a bandaid?

Look, I'm not buying that the atheists' altruistic self-professed pursuit of reason is what undergirds their conclusion that God does not exist; I believe it's because they want to believe that they'll never be called into eternal accountability for their temporal actions by a holy God. Talk about an opiate for the masses!

But to heck with what I think, eh? I'm just a hayseed, cross-eyed Christian with an IQ of 50 who believes in Jesus, loves his mama, salutes the flag and collects guns. I'm an idiot. Let's go to the atheists and hear it from the horse's mouth—or backside (411 taken from D'Souza's book, *What's So Great About Christianity*):

- Biologist Stephen Jay Gould: "We may yearn for a higher answer—but none exists. This explanation, though superficially troubling if not terrifying, is ultimately liberating and exhilarating."
- Biologist Julian Huxley, the grandson of Darwin's buddy and ally Thomas Henry Huxley, put it this way: "The sense of spiritual relief which comes from rejecting the idea of God as a supernatural being is enormous."
- Julian's brother Aldous Huxley, not to be outdone by his bro, stated, "I had motives for not wanting the world to have meaning; consequently I assumed that it had none, and was able without any difficulty to find satisfying reasons for this assumption . . . For myself as no doubt for most of my contemporaries, the philosophy of meaninglessness was essentially an instrument of liberation . . . liberation from a certain system of morality. We objected to the morality because it interfered with our sexual freedom."
- Bertrand Russell: "The worst feature of the Christian religion is its attitude toward sex."
- Christopher Hitchens: "The divorce between the sexual life and fear . . . can now at last be attempted on the sole condition that we banish all religions from the discourse."

Sounds like these atheist apostles are simply putting a nuevo twist on an ancient bent. They appear to be humming the Marquis de Sade's tune more than Sagan's. Looks and sounds like a moral revolt to me. Yes, this is Epicurus all over again.

You remember Epi, don't cha? His whole goal was to "get rid of the gods." He and his other pre-Socratic "thinkers" like Lucretius and Democritus didn't like all that duty and responsibility to higher powers and fellow mortals crap. It put a hitch in their get along. It brought them pain and they liked pleasure. They believed that such an obligation to men and the gods caused too much anxiety. They didn't like the thought of being responsible and having to account for their lives in the afterlife. Such thoughts really screwed with getting their groove on, ya know what I'm sayin'?

They were the first metrosexuals. Yep, they figured that if they could just get the gods out of the way they could focus on selfishly milking this life for all it's worth and then die without any eternal repercussions. They were living in a material world, and they were material girls. Pretty ballsy. Or stupid. But at least they were honest about their motivations.

In addition, ladies, Darwin didn't lose his faith because he discovered natural selection; he dumped God because he couldn't stomach the doctrine of eternal accountability and damnation. That's what made him switch teams. I think that was about ten years after he had married his first cousin. Git-R-Done, Charlie!

Y'know, Karl Marx said religion is the "opiate of the masses." I think the real poppy derivative is the black tar belief that tells you atheist lads and lasses that when you take the big dirt nap that's it. Ah what peace. What a high. No God. No accountability. All our sins of commission and omission will never ever come up again. No pain. No penalty.

No heaven. No hell. Imagine. Yeah, dude. Hold that hit. Let it out slowly. Ahhh. Feel better?
　　There's your opium.

Chapter 24.

How Not to be A Cho Seung Hui
(Written April 28th, 2007)

This past week Sheryl Crow instructed us all on how we could save our planet: namely, by wiping our Chattahoochee canal with only one sheet of toilet paper. Sheryl, if you really want to cool the earth, really commit and don't use any TP. If you truly believe the specious global warming doo-doo, Sher, then none has got to be better than one. Go commando, Crow!

Not being an aging, pot smoking hippie—but a very concerned dad—I think we should be showing young adults how not to be a Cho Seung Hui. Call me unhip, but I'm more concerned about how we can wipe a would-be Cho off the planet than I am about how a single ply of Charmin helps regulate the earth's surface temperatures, thereby saving the polar bear. Which reminds me, I still didn't get my polar bear permit for this fall's hunt.

The video left by Cho affords great insight into this sick gnat's psyche, which provides us with a good blueprint on how not to become twisted and pathetic. Three principle evils repeatedly showed up in this petty ninja turtle's video montage:

1. Self pity. One thing that came screaming out of the Cho video was this little wussie's "poor me" mentality. Poor

widdle Cho. Nobody likey you? You've got a rough life. This young man suffered from all the injustices of an upper middle class life: iPods, high speed internet service, the ability to attend a stellar university in a first world country with enough surplus cash to buy a frickin' arsenal and employ a stripper to entertain him in a hotel room. If only American Idol's execs would have found out about Seung's sad subsistence they could have held a telethon just for him to relieve his stress, which far outweighs what others are suffering in third world countries . . . Not.

If you, the young person, do not want to get anywhere close to being a Cho Seung Weed, then drop the pathetic waa waa stuff now. You live in America, dammit. You're blessed no matter how much your life might temporarily reek. Grow up. People across America, join me in doing this: When one of our young citizens starts a pity party in our presence, let's take the toilet paper we're now saving (thanks to Sheryl Crow) and cram it down the ungrateful narcissist's whining pie hole.

2. Blameshifting. Cho, the feeble blowhard, said Mercedes Benz, cognac, rich kids and hedonism forced his hand to kill people. Cho, if you can hear me through all the screaming you're doing in hell right now, why didn't you join the chunky and demented Rosie O'Donnell and blame Christianity and President Bush, as well?

Young person, to avoid a meet and greet with Seung Hui in Satan's sulphur pit, quit blaming others for your actions. People who do that sound like dismal weasels. Look, if circumstances (or your own terrible choices) toss you into dire straits, put on your thinking cap and try to figure how you can best field this bad deal. And in the meantime, suck it up, play the man, cease the sniveling, find the high road in your SNAFU and blow us all away by turning your lemon into lemonade—alright, Puss-N-Boots?

3. Isolation. Young person, if you don't want to think freaky thoughts that lead to doing foul things, then quit being a loner. Most people get weird when they spend too much time alone. I understand the need to be by yourself. I like my alone time, too. I need it. When alone I pray, read Scripture or other great books, enjoy a nice cigar, and I sing AC/DC songs at the top of my lungs while wearing a Spartan outfit from the movie *300*. But I've learned through years of practiced solitude that there are a few telltale signs indicating I need to cease from my solo time and become more social:
- When my seclusion begins to spawn convoluted conspiracy theories.
- When I believe my dog Spunky is commanding me, in Spanish, to start a revolution.
- When I begin to think that I am the prophet Elijah that is to precede Christ in his Second Coming, etc.

Cho went loopy being a loner. That crazy bastard did not have people around him to tell him he was a crazy bastard because he was a crazy bastard who drove off non crazy bastards. Young person, you can get unweird by getting out more often. Be friendly. Take the rejection chip off your shoulder. Buy *The Idiot's Guide to Not Being a Jerk* and get a few buddies who feel the love, freedom and responsibility to crow bar you away from your demons when they manifest—alright?

If our young ones would just suck in their pouty lip, cease to blame others because their life blows and do the Rodney King and try to get along, we could circumvent a lot of egregious behavior—not to mention Cho-like murderous mayhem.

Chapter 25.

10 Steps to Becoming an Effective Conservative Campus Hell Razer

Guess what, freshman conservative college student? In a couple of weeks you're going to have your liberal campus and its professors shove more crap down your throat than Rosie does her gullet during Chili's Monday Night Nacho Monster Blowout Special, that's what.

Are you ready?

Now, I'm not trying to make you fearful, sweetie. I just want you to brace for the liberal Kool-Aid crunch that is coming soon to a classroom near you. The stuff mommy warned you about is true. The reality is you are entering the Liberal's madrasah. Your values, for the next four years, will be violated much like Linsday Lohan's nose, liver, Mercedes and panties have been for the last five years.

Given this milieu, you have essentially three options to choose from when you're confronted with the liberal hooey. The options are:

1. You can drink the campus Kool Aid and do the Dhimmocratic do-si-do.
2. You can run from the conflict to a likeminded conservative ghetto group and hide on the curb with your little cowering crowd.

3. You and your concurring buddies can get prepped and be a conservative crew that enters campus life and joyfully, earnestly and courageously challenges the purveyors of the anti-American propaganda.

Door number three, as far as I'm concerned, is the only righteous choice. As I was entering my university years, I was (and still am) a kick butt and take names type of guy. Absorption and separation were not options for me (still aren't). I wanted to change things when I was at school, and I had a blast mixing it up on my campus back in the day which, by the way, has paved the way for a pretty cool life. Excuse me while I relish in the fruits of my labor . . . Okay, I'm back.

Look, given the slop the US is currently saddled with, if you, the young person, have an inkling of concern for our country, then an informed, entertaining and incendiary infiltration of your institute is the only answer (how's that for alliteration?). Isn't that what college and youth are all about, namely, rebellion? Isn't teenage angst all about hell raising—or in your case, hell razing? C'mon, Nancy . . . don't you want to get rowdy?

Young squab, if you are a Conservative/traditionalist then you are the rebel of our day. Yes, the times they are a changin' (have changed). "The Man" and "The Machine" on campus to rage against is not stodgy traditionalism, but rank secularism and its moral and political vacuity. Meet the new boss, James Dean.

For those new students who wish to make a dent on their campus, not only for their sake but for the following generations, I have 10 things you must get if you want to absolutely screw with the asinine screwballs at your university. To be an effective agent of change you've got to do the following:

1. Get a sense of humor. Most liberal profs and student activists are a screeching, nerve grating, nasally bunch of

whiners. As a matter of fact, I'd rather watch Janet Reno do jumping jacks and hack squats in Borat's thong than listen to the hemp clothed, goatee bearing, chunky liberal bleat.

Therefore, conservative student, when you queue up to address your crowd, be pleasant, poke fun at yourself, remove the whine from your voice and use honed humor to humiliate the Left. Getting folks to laugh at your opponents and not being rabid about taking yourself so seriously helps get your point across. To upgrade your general funniness, get Judy Carter's book, *Stand Up Comedy*.

2. Get creative. God bless technology. Conservative rebels, you have at your fingertips the wherewithal to go creatively crazy for the cause of God and country with the real possibility of a stack of people seeing and hearing what you have got to offer.

Therefore, get nutty with your stuff. Utilize these amazing techno tools to tackle the tools on the left. Take your gift, your talent, your voice and your God-wired weirdness and, every now and then, put something artistic out there that'll overtly or covertly slam dance the secularists who seek to sabotage our society. To upgrade your competitive creativity get *Chasing Cool,* by Noah Kerner and Gene Pressman.

3. Get tough. One thing that drives me nuts about some Sallys on the right is their bemoaning how they get attacked when they go public in the classroom with their sentiments. Whaa! What did you think the Ward Churchills were going to do, clap? Buy you candy? Wash your undercarriage? Look, not-so-sharp-holder-of-traditional-values, we're in a very real culture war. The _ _ _ _ will hit the fan when you counter the liberal crud in the classroom. Embrace it. Suck it up. Get tough. Let adversity be your Wheaties, the breakfast of champions! If you want to upgrade your resiliency, get my book, *The Bulldog Attitude: Get It or Get Left Behind*.

4. Get prayerful. Most folks on the ludicrous left who embrace what 21st century Dhimmocrats currently spew are

admitted atheists. Seeing that they don't believe in the God who is, I'm a guessin' they are probably not down the funnel with the discipline of prayer. That is, until they're about to die. Then, of course, they start praying like Chris Tucker freshly filled with the Holy Ghost and fire. Since they refuse to believe and pray to God, they have no supernatural help in their hapless cause. At least no positive supernatural help because we all know demons love to assist these guys. But I digress . . .

The traditionalist (usually) believes in the God of Scripture . . . the God who's got a will and way that He'd like to see implemented on the planet. This is cool; however, God follower, take it to the next level and start praying with faith and oomph for His will to be done on earth as it is in heaven (this includes your campus).

So . . . God-fearing traditionalist, ask God for a) crazy clout to change yourself so that you're not a waste-oid He's got to work around and b) for a dynamic enabling to effect constructive change on your campus and culture. To upgrade your prayer life, get E. M. Bounds' classic, *Power Through Prayer*.

5. Get rebellious. When rebels see what "everyone else is doing," they usually shoot it the finger and do the opposite. They know that more than likely there must be something fundamentally wrong with "it" if everyone thinks it is mondo jovial. Especially if many of the adherents of the en masse mantra put the funk in dysfunction.

At today's universities, college student, you will be a radical if you don't lock step to the secularization, slutification and wussification that these institutions and their devotees try to cram up your and America's backside. So, put on your leather jacket, grab a nice cigar, climb on your Von Dutch and tell these God-, country-, goodness- and common sense-haters to get bent. Go against the grain. Stand alone if you have to. To upgrade your rebel yell, read *Rosa Parks:*

My Story, by Rosa Parks, listen to some Godsmack and stand tall.

    6. Get informed. Conservative contrarians, you've got to get the following books and read them:

The Politically Incorrect Guide to American History,
The Politically Incorrect Guide to Darwinism and Intelligent Design,
The Politically Incorrect Guide to English and American Literature,
The Politically Incorrect Guide to Global Warming and Environmentalism,
The Politically Incorrect Guide to Islam (and the Crusades),
The Politically Incorrect Guide to Science,
The Politically Incorrect Guide to the Constitution,
The Politically Incorrect Guide to the South (and Why It Will Rise Again),
The Politically Incorrect Guide to Women, Sex, and Feminism, and
Conservative Comebacks to Liberal Lies, by Gregg Jackson

Digest the above and, when appropriate, take some of the factoids found within these secularism devastating tomes and share them with your prof during class and your buddies in the dorm. It's fun for the whole family.

    7. Get speakers to your campus who'll fire up your base. Young America's Foundation has an entire smorgasbord of world-class speakers covering every conceivable topic who can deftly dismember the left's bereft beliefs. To upgrade your campus base, go to YAF.org, order one of their ideological black belts and let the party start. In addition, you can book me to speak to your group. I'd love to come and toss the cat among the pigeons. Go to ClashRadio.com/seminars, and let's yuck it up! I'll see the boys and girls at Duke in

October. I'll be talking about masculinity vs. bogus metrosexuality. Yeehaw!

8. Get sharp looking. Most campus Liberals have a monopoly on ugly. They are neither pleasing to the ear nor eye. Do not follow their lead, young conservative. If they want to look sloven, unshorn and tie-dyed let 'em. You, however, should run in the opposite direction.

Don't believe that crap about looks don't matter. The heck they don't. If I have the choice between these two options: 1) to look at and listen to an obese girl with frizzed out hair and so many piercings that it looks like a tackle box blew up in her face while she's wearing no bra with her 40DDD floppies staring right at me while she is yelling or 2) to look at and listen to a svelte, well put together, conscientious lass graciously appealing to me, I am telling you right here and now that I'll choose #2. The nasty girl has offended my senses, lost my attention, and I could not care less what she has to say. Call me crazy.

Girls, to upgrade your appearance, get *A Guide to Elegance: For Every Woman Who Wants to Be Well and Properly Dressed on All Occasions*, by Genevieve Antoine Dariaux. Guys, grab a copy of *Dressing the Man: Mastering the Art of Permanent Fashion*, by Alan Flusser, and watch the difference the clothes make.

9. Get your grades up.

10. Get your hands dirty. Serve your campus and community. The world has enough of derisive, hate-filled protests and marches by ideological miscreants. While you're in college, help in the critical areas of your campus and community's needs and watch the campus and community give you a standing O.

Chapter 26.

John Edwards Might Be Full of Crap, but Our Enemies Are Not

I'm originally from Texas where I was raised to actually believe people when they tell you something. You remember that tired old maxim that your word is your bond, don't 'cha? When I moved to Miami I was quick to discover that things were a tad bit different. In Miami, your word means nada. As a matter of fact, I've come to learn that the opposite of what people tell me (a lot of the time) is the truth. Yes, Dorothy, I am no longer in Kansas.

Now, this isn't really peculiar to South Florida, and I hate to admit, but it even happens in Texas. All of us, everywhere, say things we don't mean. When a wife asks her husband, "Do these jeans make my hips look big?" the now sweating, self-preserving spouse says a quick "no" when he's thinking "yes." The reason being? Well, he wants to continue to eat home cooked meals.

Girls lie on dates all the time. When a girl cuts a date short telling her suitor halfway through the hors d'oeuvres that she's had a nice time but must get up early the next morning for work, what she is really saying is, "Please don't kill me, you whacked out, ham-fisted crotch rocket."

Honestly, I dish the spin myself. The other day my wife's friend got a really bad haircut. They were both standing in my kitchen when said friend asked me what I thought of her new doo. I said, "It looks nice, and it is probably way more manageable," when what I was really thinking was, "Holy God . . . did you lose a bet or what?"

Insincerity plagues our speech; however, we would be unwise to think that the disingenuousness within our discourse is also part and parcel of the rhetoric of our ill-intentioned Islam (and other extreme) enemies. Yep, we'd be plain goofy to think that our enemies are just joshing or being hyperbolic when they say they want to destroy us and that for which we stand. In addition, we'd be loopy to assume that if they do mean what they say that they're just like us, and we can get them to stand down if we give them a squeaky toy.

Preening Breck Girl, John "autoerotic" Edwards, has of late, been traipsing around the U.S. telling us that the War on Terror is nothing more than a bumper sticker. John Boy takes the attacks and vents of our sworn enemies and downplays them. Edwards sees the WOT as nothing more than Republican-hyped fodder used to generate fear in order to cow their voting block to lockstep come November 4th, 2008. I guess Edwards assumes that, much like him, our radical enemies are full of BS and do not mean what they say.

People who are not like the boot lick Edwards, on the other hand, believe that radical Islam and their hate drunk ilk intend to do exactly what they say they're going to do. What do our enemies propose to do?

In his new book, *In The Words of Our Enemies*, Jed Babbin has done a great favor for all of us who do not wish to live life with our heads up our butts and has compiled an extensive and veritable one-stop shocking block of the hate speeches that have been vomited out by the tyrants and terrorists who are energetically auguring our eradication.

In Babbin's book you will read our foes' invectives before they've been scrubbed clean and Lysol disinfected by our limp-wrist, liberal pundits and "news" outlets. For instance, you'll get the skinny directly from the lunatic's laptop regarding . . .

- China's war strategy of paralyzing our computer networks and infrastructure as a precursor to a full military attack.
- Russia's unashamed declaration of its intent to sell nuclear weapons to Islamic terrorist operations.
- North Korea's blatantly false propaganda denouncing capitalism and predicting the downfall of the United States.
- Cuba's plans to collaborate with Iran to bring the United States to its knees.
- Islamist's bone-chillingly detailed campaign for the mass murder of all westerners.

Look, whether you're conservative or liberal, do yourself a favor and just read the junk that spills off the tongues of our enemies. And then ask yourself, given their history, whether they mean what they say or not.

I, for one, take Osama, Ahmadinejad, Kim Jong Il, Putin, Chavez and Hu Jintao at their word. I don't think these cats have the duplicity in their diatribes against America that we use in our verbiage with each other. I take them seriously when they say that they intend to crush us like a cockroach in Queen Latifa's house. I also believe that to think otherwise is to do so to our own detriment.

Chapter 27.

Pit Bulls and Stupid Fools

It's sad that one of the greatest dog breeds ever to grace the planet, the American Pit Bull Terrier, has fallen into the hands of animal abusing idiots. Guys like Michael Vick, our nation's scurrilous hip hop hoodlums and other waste-of-sperm-and-eggs are not even worthy to carry this canine's excrement, much less superintend their subsistence. The Pit Bulls should be walking these boys on the leash, teaching them to fetch, heel and sit and not the other way around.

I think I speak for all Pit Bull lovers by saying, "thanks morons for sullying a substantial animal's rep via dog fighting." Why don't you Darwinian holdovers get another hobby, huh ladies? I've got something you could do. Since you like doing radical stuff . . . how about bungee jumping without the bungee? Or base jumping without a 'chute? Or trying to catch bullets with your teeth? Yeah, that's it.

Of the many things that suck about Vick's and his vapid gang's Pit Bull fighting, one particular thing (aside from the obvious abuse) that ticks me off is this noble breed gets officially branded, once again, as Satan's Cerberus.

The truth of the matter is that the Pit Bull is one of the sweetest dogs that has ever schlepped this pebble, and anyone who's spent any time around a well-bred bully knows that I speak the truth. Can I get a witness, my brethren?

When I lived in Texas, I was privileged to have owned several of these fine animals. My children were raised with them from the day they came home from the hospital 'til the time we moved to Dade County, Florida which unfortunately disallows these dogs.

My Pit Bulls guarded my girls with their lives. They were my daughter's favorite playmates. Our dogs would pull their little wagons, let my girls ride them like ponies, let them dress them up in goofy outfits, all the while my dogs sat there patiently taking it with a big Pit Bull grin on their faces.

At night my bullies would lay at my little ladies' feet, protecting them as they simultaneously rested and recharged their batteries so they could wake up the next day and conquer the earth all over again.

Pit Bulls vicious? I don't think so. Not mine. Not unless you really pushed them or threatened our family. If you were dumb enough to do that, then you got the message real quick from our pups that you were about to meet Jesus if you did not cease and desist.

Our dogs were more like comedians than commandos. They showed zero unwarranted aggression toward people and pooches. They had amazing discernment, insane athletic ability and undaunted courage. This breed impacted me so much I wrote a book about their magnificent spirit (check amazon.com for *The Bulldog Attitude*).

As far as I'm concerned, the Pit Bull is one of the most awesome animals on the planet. And before the pimps and thugs became the owners of this noble animal and hype hit the fan and the local news needed fresh chum for the gullible ones, The United States of America thought so as well. Yes, the U.S. believed that the Pit Bull was great enough to be our mascot in World War One. During WWI, Life magazine frequently had Pit Bulls on their covers and in their cartoons, using them as a symbol of America's stalwart spirit.

In Jacqueline O'Neil's book, *The American Pit Bull Terrier*, Jackie brings out the fact that a Pit Bull named Stubby was the war's outstanding canine soldier. He earned the rank of Sergeant, was mentioned in official dispatches and earned two medals—one for warning of a gas attack and the other for holding a German spy at bay at Chemin des Dames until American troops arrived.

In addition, the Pit Bull was also one of our nation's beloved canine movie stars. Remember, the Our Gang and Little Rascals comedy series with Spanky, Alfalfa, Darla and Buckwheat? Do you remember their dog, Pete? He was a Pit Bull (actually, they used ten different Pit Bulls for the show). Did Pete eat any of the cast of the show? No. Was he cool, tolerant, funny and well-behaved as the Little Rascals used him to pull their wagons, do their tricks and run their errands? Yes.

Historically speaking, it was not the pimps and thugs or the foolishly overpaid, depraved athletes and empty entertainers who owned these dogs. Matter of fact, some of our most famous folks were fanciers of the Pit Bull, namely Thomas Edison, Helen Keller, President Theodore Roosevelt, Jack Dempsey and Fred Astaire.

As you can tell my affection and esteem for this animal is sky high. My dogs were amazing. It sickens me to think that because of some goof's desire to make some cash off a dog fight, or his desire to posture himself as some tough guy, or his wet dream of being just like the guy he saw on MTV, that this brilliant breed walks away with a black eye. I say lets give the black eye to the bad guy who abuses a Pit Bull and leave the dog alone.

Chapter 28.

Traditionalists Don't Wear ButtSmacker Lip Balm

For the last 40 years, there has been a belligerent, systematic secularization of the United States by the liberal thought cops. These individuals have sought to remove from all public sectors of society any semblance of biblical values, all influence of religious institutions, all sacred symbolism and the traditional core values which have made America great.

A myopic Cyclops can see this.

Of the many mental things the secularist suffers from, two primary pains motivate them to work against the universe: 1) a repulsion from God and 2) a massive American History memory loss.

Being saddled with these sicknesses, instead of seeking healing or having an exorcism or joining MA (Misguided Anonymous) or just moving to Holland where they'll be nice and comfy, they have chosen rather to create a new United States of Sassy Secularists in which the traditionalist is kicked to the curb and their novel material girls get to govern.

To accomplish the creation of the USSS, they have become busy monkeys trying to level authorities, rewrite records, become judge and jury of all things everywhere, homogenize cultures, pimp style over substance and deify power while they prop up the "victims of the system" to drive their imagined American magic bus.

On Planet Secularity where truth is dead, muscle-power becomes the operative standard of speech. The results are cultic conformity and group bullying. The chief orgasmic goal of the secular sellers of societal swill is to create a rock-solid environment of political correctness—with the intended end being the cowing of people who might rustle their feathers by not parroting their already tried (and been found wanting) opinions. They can't allow people to speak and free think because the realist and the truth dealer would pee on their little party.

Therefore, the person who champions a traditional view of truth (not propaganda), who stands for the historical record (not the hysterical read) and who believes that biblically-based, previously proven and transcendent standards should continue to serve as an external pattern to govern our nation's character will endure more scorn than Ted Nugent, Rush Limbaugh and me crashing Rosie's "Lesbians Only" plus size pool party. But that doesn't rattle the God and country lover's cage.

The faithful traditionalist who loves God and the way this nation was originally constituted will stand up against this hijacking of our nation by the secularists. Yes, the grand and the noble will not lie down and roll up like an opossum just because the truth isn't en vogue. Great people side with truth even when it's detested.

The traditionalist who's worth his salt will not put on ButtSmacker lip balm and kiss the chunky backside of the secularists when they jam it in his face for an acquiescing smooch. No sir. No way. Not now. Not ever.

Rather, the hardy traditionalist, while humming the words to Twisted Sister's hit song, "We're Not Gonna Take It," will continue to speak out, work hard and self sacrifice in order to preserve classic traditional America values.

Chapter 29.

The Islam-O-Fascists Must be Happier Than a Pig in Fresh Mud

The Islam-O-Fascists must be happier than a pig in fresh mud as they watch our nation become more cleaved than Pam Anderson's hooters. I'm certain the terrorists, both here and abroad, are having a good jihadic giggle over a smoldering hookah as they view our wilting will to war.

Yeah, I bet Bin Laden is blowing blond Lebanese smoke rings right now as his group regroups with fresh enthusiasm regarding how they can kill us while we're embroiled in a divisive, political whizzing match over what to do with people who want to kill us. They are probably sharpening their scimitars on their whet stones even as I write this, while some of their thicker ones try on their new suicide bomber jackets and still others wait for FedEx to deliver a fresh supply of plutonium to their Afghani bat cave.

As a conservative, I've got issues that are obviously very important to me . . . stuff that I'll fight over, split over—and a couple I'll die/kill for; however, my primary concern since 9/11 is that we continue to have a nation to debate and divide in.

Sure, I want my presidential vote-getter to be on the same page as me and my many issues. As a matter of fact, I'd like him to hire me as one of his top advisors and supply me with an all access pass to the White House gun room, cigar lounge and mini bar. But since the Islamic radical butt monkeys attacked us five+ years ago and are currently conjuring up ways to eclipse their last assault, the main thing I'm looking for in America's next el Capitan is that he will crush those who are trying to end this great American experiment and will do it on their turf and on our terms.

This means I'm not voting by looks, smoothness or pet political peripheral obsessions. I am officially a one-issue man this go round. The issue that drives me now is our country's right to life.

I don't care if the next president . . .
- has excellent hair or a bad comb over,
- grins 'til his teeth are dry or looks ticked off all the time,
- has superior body language or blinks too much,
- spends $400 or $4 to cut his graying follicles,
- is Mormon, Methodist or Martian,
- has been married one time or three,
- has kids who love him or who hate him,
- has a big carbon footprint
- is telegenic or has a face made for radio, and lastly,
- believes to the "T" everything about life and marriage I believe.

Frankly Scarlet, I don't give a damn. Ok, it's not that I don't give a damn, it's just that what I'm concerned about is very specific: What I need to know is whether the next president elect will keep us protected and seek to throttle those who wish to whittle or nation down to nothing. Primarily, I'm looking for a president who understands how deeply we are hated by radical Islam and what a constant threat they're going to be to us 'til Christ returns, and one who will effectively mitigate them during his term(s) via diplomacy—and if that doesn't work, then by death.

Chapter 30.

Teachers Should Pack in Case Students are Attacked
(Written October 13th, 2007)

"Should properly trained and licensed teachers be allowed to carry guns into their classrooms?" That's the $64k question being tossed around this week (once again) after Satan's latest spawn, Asa Coon, stooge emeritus, decided to shoot up his Cleveland high school's teachers and classmates this week. How about, yes teachers should be allowed to lock and load because not being able to doesn't seem to be working.

As far as I'm concerned, a responsible and trained teacher should ab-so-frickin'-lutely be able to carry on campus. And none of this "concealed weapons" crap. I'm talking about visibly carrying their piece on their hip. And not just one but two massive nickel-plated S&W Model 29 .44 magnums with 7 1/2 inch barrels with bandoliers thrown around their shoulders, and next to their juicy apple and pencil jar on their desk they should have a mounted .50 cal. machine gun. You know . . . "just in case."

If that's too much, I think, at least, all first year teachers should go through Jason Bourne-like weapons training and be issued a 9mm Glock upon signing their contract with a new school. Kind of a "Welcome to the Jungle, glad to have you" gift.

If I taught school, not only would I want to carry a gun into class in order to stop (please read kill) a pathetic punk who's decided he's going to mass murder twenty-three of his peers because two of them made fun of his chartreuse doo rag in his latest Facebook profile photo.

I'd also have on me for lesser offenses:
- An 8ft. bullwhip to peel the flesh from the backs of the multitudinous smarmy adolescent smart alecks
- Throwing knives for persistent cheaters
- Brass knuckles for the morons who call someone's precious daughter a b*tch, slut or whore
- Concussion grenades to break up the bathroom orgies
- A night stick for the Boulder High School admin monkeys who tell students that ecstasy, weed and screwing everything that moves is okay. And lastly, I'd have . . .
- Desks that would flip backwards, dumping the student who just told me to f— off into an underground water tank filled with sharks with lasers on their heads.

In short, my classsroom would look like Van Helsing's house. No one would dare try anything. It would be the safest place on the planet. Parents would love it.

Yep, it seems as if the formerly nice and quaint public schools of yesteryear have officially come to resemble in character, intelligence, morality and safety our nation's prison systems. Especially where I live in South Florida. Heck, they look and operate like jails. They're ridiculously over-crowded with aspiring criminals sporting entitlement mentalities who are fueled on violence, disdain, sexual weirdness and Mountain Dew.

Teachers Should Pack in Case Students are Attacked

Then there's the tasteless architecture of the school itself with its assiduously strewn barb wire, sprinkling of squad cars wedged up against the exit doors, and the soft, gentle pinging of metal detectors at the entrance. All of it screams jail to me. I say we might as well arm the guards, I mean, the teachers.

You know what's weird? When I grew up in Texas we regularly brought our guns to school with us, especially during hunting season. And you know what else? We made fun of each other, we had rough days, and we got into fights. And no one . . . with weapons all around . . . ever brandished a gun and started strafing the crowd. If we had a problem we'd walk into a nearby alley and beat the snot out of each other. It was a beautiful thing. No guns. Just fists of fury. And usually after the scrap the combatants became compadres.

Also, back in the day, the teachers weren't scared of us. They beat us. My coach, principle, choir and shop teacher would beat the white off my butt when I got out of line. No students went home and got their crack head uncle's .25 auto and came back and shot the teachers and/or the students. But that day is long gone, and ever since we yanked corporal punishment and teacher terror out of the classroom room we've had a spike in dead students and faculty.

Finally, I'm a guessin' that 99.9% of the parents who lost their children in the following wish that their child's teacher had a gun in order to defend their now deceased child:
- Stockton massacre – Stockton, California, January 17, 1989
- University of Iowa shooting - Iowa City, Iowa, November 1, 1991
- Simon's Rock College of Bard shooting - Great Barrington, Massachusetts, December 14, 1992
- East Carter High School shooting - Grayson, Kentucky, January 18, 1993

- Richland High School shooting - Lynnville, Tennessee, November 15, 1995
- Frontier Junior High shooting - Moses Lake, Washington, February 2, 1996
- Pearl High School shooting - Pearl, Mississippi, October 1, 1997
- Heath High School shooting - West Paducah, Kentucky, December 1, 1997
- Jonesboro massacre - Jonesboro, Arkansas, March 24, 1998
- Thurston High School shooting - Springfield, Oregon, May 21, 1998
- Columbine High School massacre - near Littleton, Colorado, April 20, 1999
- Heritage High School shooting - Conyers, Georgia, May 20, 1999
- Santana High School - Santee, California, March 5, 2001
- Appalachian School of Law shooting - Grundy, Virginia, January 16, 2002
- Rocori High School shootings - Cold Spring, Minnesota, September 24, 2003
- Red Lake High School massacre - Red Lake, Minnesota, March 21, 2005
- Campbell County High School - Jacksboro, Tennessee, November 8, 2005
- Platte Canyon High School shooting - Bailey, Colorado, September 27, 2006
- Weston High School shooting - Cazenovia, Wisconsin September 29, 2006
- Amish school shooting - Nickel Mines, Lancaster County, Pennsylvania, October 2, 2006
- Henry Foss High School - Tacoma, Washington, January 3, 2007

- Virginia Tech massacre - Blacksburg, Virginia, April 16, 2007
- SuccessTech Academy shooting - Cleveland, Ohio, October 10, 2007

We can't afford to rely on chunky security guards with golf carts, pepper spray, whistles and plastic badges to safeguard against these armed little death dealing bastards from hell (I believe the security guard at SuccessTech was on vacation when Coon attempted to kill his mates).

The reality is that this stuff goes down when you least expect it, and as long as schools don't have some armed teachers and faculty who have been properly trained and equipped to kill the post-pubescent perps, the more we will continue to carry innocent children out of their classrooms in black body bags. Call me weird, but in every school shooting there should be only one casualty, namely the gun wielding culprit who commenced the chaos, and not your bystanding book carrying kid.

Chapter 31.

Eyes, Ears, Nose, Throat and Car Bombs? (Written July 7th, 2007)

Evidently the Muslim doctors who were busted in last week's UK terrorist attacks aren't cool with the Hippocratic Oath like our western Marcus Welbys are. These stethoscope-donning wannabe dealers of death seem to have no problem in trying to heal us on Tuesday morning and kill us at Tiger Tiger on Friday night. Their Mr. McDreamy is very McDeadly.

Hey, didn't you just love the spin spun last weekend from the various news agencies across the pond regarding the origins of these monstrous MDs? We were told that these tools were "Asians." Asians?

I'm thinking ... have the Japanese gone and attacked our snaggle-toothed brethren? No?

Has some Fu Man Choo from China begun to give our allies the big fongool? Strike two?

I know ... those sweet old Tibetan monks have now broken bank and gone bonkers on Great Britain? I always knew that whole "peace and love stuff" they were selling was a bunch of crap. No, not them either? So, if it wasn't Japan, China or Tibet—then who was it?

Was it the Mongolians, North Koreans, Vietnamese, East Timorites—or was it a bunch of Dr. Evils from Laos! What? I'm not even close? Dang it!

I know . . . you guys were probably talking about the rock band, Asia? That's it. Did Downes, Wetton, Howe and Palmer become terrorists after their third album tanked in '85? Is that whodunit? No? Crap! What people group are you talkin' about when you say the culprits were "Asian?"

What's that? You say the terrorists were from western Asia? Oh, okay. However, most people who live not in the land of BSville normally just call "Western Asians" who try to kill people with gasoline and buckets of nails "Middle Eastern Muslim radicals."

Asian? Please.

Not only did our cousins get attacked by "Western Asians" but, as stated, the dudes who attempted to slay our friends were their doctors. Uh oh. The terrorist profile just got expanded.

No longer are the Islamic pain in the asses the 18-year old, chronically unemployed, nanny goat bearded bomb tossers who wear a pillow case for a hat, but now, in the west, they're wearing scrubs and sporting tongue depressors. And they can write a prescription for life or death. The terrorists, like the Jeffersons, seem to be movin' on up. Yes, now we're singing the white collared blues.

What a test for England's new Prime Minister Gordon Brown, eh? It seems as if Brown is playing this rough hand well. He's announced that he's going to look into the backgrounds of all the highly-skilled migrant workers entering the United Kingdom like Al Gore's kid would examine a fresh quarter pound of red haired skunk weed.

Mr. Brown also said he was ready to look at Conservative proposals for a national border police force and consider a call from David Cameron for a ban on Muslim political party Hizb-ut-Tahrir. Giddy up, Brown. Good for you. Perhaps you can cease the British bulldog from its present morphing into a capitulating poodle to these problematic people.

You've got a tough row to hoe, Mr. Brown. My prayers are with you. With tens of thousands of Islamic radical whack jobs within your borders who are just jiffy with jihad, and with Mohammed being the second most popular name for new "British" baby boys born in '07, it seems as if you have one mell of hess on your hands.

So, Prime Minister, tap into the spirit of Winston Churchill. Grow some 'nads the size of Texas. Investigate each and every cleric, doctor, lawyer, business owner and rebel teen you might feel the slightest inkling doesn't salute your Union Jack and that for which it stands. And for God's sake, please have your reporters and your pundits stop saying "Asian" when you mean "Middle Eastern radical Muslims."

Chapter 32.

Get Britney a Gun and Teach Her to Hunt

If I hung around all the Beavises in close proximity to Britney Spears and those Anna Nicole was unfortunate enough to schlep with and Hollywood was my reality, I too, would:
1. shave my head,
2. be wasted during awards shows,
3. stay completely blitzed out of my brain on dope,
4. tattoo every square inch of my noggin,
5. pierce, not just my ears, but the front part of my brain,
6. pummel parked cars with umbrellas.

I know I have a black belt in being a loveless jerk; however, I can empathize with their extreme behavior and their indulgence into mind-altering drugs. If I were forced into their situation and had to listen to Bobby Trendy, Howard K. Stern, KFed and Paris's stuff 24/7, I would take bong hits morning, noon and night, mainline Ketel One and drink methadone like it was Yoo Hoo. If not, I'm afraid that I'd be up on murder charges, as I lean more toward being homicidal than suicidal.

Thankfully, drugs, an early grave and murder are not the only option for Brit (or any other girl caught in similar circumstances). One thing you young ladies could do is take responsibility and climb out of that toilet you've gotten yourself into, and muy pronto. That's right, leave your "friends" now. All of them. Including your family, if they have aided and abetted your asininity. Do it. Wherever you are . . . go! Just take off running in the opposite direction, even if that means into heavy traffic on the 405. Dodging multiple high speed moving vehicles is safer than hanging with the warped monkeys you're around now.

Most folks would say you Britney-types need to go to rehab. I'm all about going to rehab. I'm in rehab right now. I'm trying to get delivered from my acerbic Left loathing, my metrosexual nausea, my America loving, my gun collecting, my God worshipping and my testosterone addictions that the secular progressives say are "wrong." It's not going very well. I keep on falling off the wagon. Or is it falling on the wagon? Whatever it is, I'm not getting "better." Anyway, this is not about me and my angst. My advice for you, Brit (and those mired in similar Shiite), is not to check into rehab but dive into hunting. This is easy math.

Check it out: Hollywood hates guns, hunting and eating meat, and they spit out the daftest characters on the planet. Therefore, if you girls don't want to be Tinseltown divorced multiple times, plastic surgery addicted, booze and dope dependant STD machines, you've got to do the opposite of what Hollywood does; i.e., get into guns, hunting and eating meat. It's logical. My grad school profs would be proud of that deduction . . . I think.

I've noticed in my wonderful world of guns and hunting that we don't have too many drug and alcohol addled freak boys and girls. Sure, there are one or two helix misers in our humongous community, but we pale in comparison to Hollywood's glut of Darwinian throwbacks. It seems as if the bang of the gun, the flight of the arrow and the thrill of the hunt are effective in keeping one's feet tethered to the planet.

I believe that just as you emasculate a man when you remove him from the wild, you slay a woman when she doesn't get a regular dose of the primal scream of nature—in particular, the hunt. Girls, hunting is an escape and a sensual exchange that getting new hip implants, maxing out a Master Card, and having a porn video made of you and your boyfriend's ham fisted love-making attempts could never outdo.

Hey, nutty college chick, you wannabe a "Girl Gone Wild?" Well, good. Women, like men, are born to be wild. Having an undomesticated feral facet to your life is right, and I believe that when you girls do not get a regular release of this rebel yell/huntress/outdoor otherness, you're going to seek out some artificial, and oft times damaging, sensory satisfaction.

If you like thrills and chills, I'm talkin' wacky, hair standing up on end, slap your momma, OMG stuff that blows away anything chemicals or herbs can provide, try this:

1. Hunt a grizzly bear with a recurve bow.
2. Go to Africa and stare down a cape buffalo, an elephant or a rogue bull hippo (out of the water) armed only with an old British double rifle.
3. Bound through an alligator and water moccasin infested swamp chasing a perturbed wild boar.
4. Run over the desert mountains of Arizona following dogs that are hot on the trail of a mountain lion.
5. Try, just try, to sneak up on a mature whitetail buck or a giant kudu bull. I bet you can't get within 1oo yards before he shows you his backside and then leaves you in the dust.
6. Fight with a 500-lb bull shark, a 150-lb tarpon, a 7-ft sailfish or a 40-lb. mahi-mahi.

The above is true also for the young women who don't strip, do sex tapes, aren't drug dependant or dating backup dancers for boy bands. You, too, can be imbalanced and a candidate for a meltdown (though probably less sensational than Brit's) if you don't get out of your regular world of bland and get dirty in the hunt.

It seems like more and more women are catching onto the buzz that is hunting. Thanks to Safari Club International and their Sables sub-division, the Becoming an Outdoors-Woman organization, the beautiful huntress Cindy Garrison and her TV show, the equally gorgeous Shemane Nugent's example and Fiona Capstick's amazing book, *The Diana Files: The Huntress – Traveler Through History*, the ladies are leaving that which is plastic and entering into that which truly satisfies: the hunt. I almost forgot to mention this, but major labels are coming out with safari clothes for girls so that you can look hot in the field. PTL!

Many women are following their men into the countryside. They, too, want to see sunsets and sunrises, breathe fresh air, see stars, get scared, enjoy a campfire, pursue game, feel the rush, eat the flesh, chew leather and truly get wild—but without the nonsense.

". . . we need to conserve that bitter impulse that we have inherited from primitive man. It alone permits us the greatest luxury of all, the ability to enjoy a vacation from the human condition through an authentic, 'immersion in Nature' . . . and this, in turn, can be achieved only by placing himself in relation to another animal. But there is no animal, pure animal, other than a wild one, and the relationship with him is the hunt." - Jose Ortega y Gasset.

Chapter 33.

A Sanctuary for Demoniacs

I have nothing against friendly foreigners who want to get the heck out of their banana republic and get a legal life over here in the land of plenty. I feel your pain, hombres. Well, not really. Actually, I have no idea what kind of gruel you have to slog through while I live on a marina in Miami next to a world-class golf course.

God bless America. God bless the American Dream.

However, given the fact that you're leaving your homeland in flippin' droves, I'm guessin' the place sucks like a ravenous Rosie working the fleshy remnants of a ripe mango seed.

Look, if I were a Mexican living in Mexico, I too would be braving long walks through the desert and even swimming across the Rio Grande during flood stage. Why? There are three reasons:

1. American TV is better. Have you seen the horrid Mexican stuff they torture their citizens with?
2. I'd get sick of mariachis playing their big guitars and singing through their noses at me in restaurants. I like peace and quiet when I eat an enchilada with my lady. I don't want three chunky Julios butchering their guitars in my face, singing "Frito Bandito" at

the top of their lungs while I'm masticating with my Maria in public. Comprende?
3. I want some money, honey. I'd be running north to the States through Gila monsters, prickly pear and javelinas, because after about a year of living La Vida Broka, I'd like to earn some real cash, dammit. Getting paid in drinking gourds, chickens and corn tortillas after pouring concrete for 18 hours a day in 119 degree heat would get real old muy quickly.

Yes, I would be looking across the border for the bigger, better deal for me and mi casa if I were an upright Mexican with kids to take care of. Who can blame them?

I'd also be looking to relocate to the States if I were a punk criminal/piece of Samsonite/worthless scum bucket/Darwinian holdover from anywhere in the world. Why? It's quite obvious. America has more stuff and better stuff for the criminal's clutches. Look, sombrero and donkey theft in Guadalajara is only fun for the first two, maybe three times, and after that the buzz wears thin. In America, however, there are all kinds of toys to steal and plenty of people, places and things to use and abuse. In some cities if we catch you, the illegal alien, we won't even report you or deport you. Isn't that yummy?

However, you must be careful, you chunk of thieving, raping, killing and gang-bangin' crud, that you stay in a "Sanctuary City." Indeed, in order to have a long and successful life of crime here in the United States of Anarchy, you, the felonious illegal freak, have to choose with precision the places to prey upon our people. If you don't, you could (if caught in some municipalities) get sent back to Suckville and the old donkey thieving, mariachis and Mexican soap opera schlock. And you wouldn't want that to happen now would you, señor?

A Sanctuary for Demoniacs

To help you in your evil and illegal existence here in the States, herewith is a partial list of craven, criminal-assisting cities to inhabit in order for you to carry out dirty deeds:
Anchorage, Alaska
Fairbanks, Alaska
Chandler, Arizona
Fresno, California
Los Angeles, California
San Diego, California
San Francisco, California
Sonoma County, California
Evanston, Illinois
Cicero, Illinois
Cambridge, Massachusetts
Orleans, Massachusetts
Portland, Maine
Baltimore, Maryland
Takoma Park, Maryland
Ann Arbor, Michigan
Minneapolis, Minnesota
Durham, North Carolina
Albuquerque, New Mexico
Aztec, New Mexico
Rio Arriba County, New Mexico
Santa Fe, New Mexico
New York, New York
Ashland, Oregon
Gaston, Oregon
Marion County, Oregon
Austin, Texas
Houston, Texas
Katy, Texas
Seattle, Washington
Madison, Wisconsin

If arrested here, never fear; the local authorities won't even ask you where you are from and if you are legal. You will not be deported. It's a satanic dream-come-true for you poor little darlings.

Rest assured, demoniacs, that the Mayor McCheeses who lord over the sanctuary cities promise you the following if you get busted: no deportation and outrageously cheap bail. If convicted, they guarantee you stupidly short sentences, a nice education, some soft porn on cable, three squares a day, plus Pilates classes and . . . and . . . when you get out . . . they'll let you stay in their city where you can screw them and us all over again.

Chapter 34.

It's Time for Conservatives to Take Comedy Seriously

I know I'm not supposed to say this as a conservative and as a Christian, but Steve Colbert, John Stewart, David Letterman, Carlos Mencia, Dave Chappelle and Bill Maher are funny hombres. Even though I radically and fundamentally disagree with most of their content, funny is as funny does. They're like farts. Most folks don't really like farts, but farts are funny. Period. Especially when it's yours and it's silent.

Look, as far as comedy goes, Mr. and Mrs. Conservative, you must bow and kiss the Left's ring. They slay us. You can count on one hand how many conservatives are making a semi-distinct blip on the comedic scene. Who do we have? Dennis Miller, Brad Stine, Julie Gorin, and _____ . I had to google "conservative comics" just to add a third person to that list.

Why can't conservatives get their comedic act together? The liberals, on a 24/7 basis, are tossing us soft balls that we should be driving out of the park in a humorous prime time way. It's so easy it's stupid. All we have to do is just read the crap that the left does, out loud, and it's hilarious. We don't even have to be that imaginative and try to develop quips, as they provide an endless supply of ammunition. We couldn't make up the stuff they do even if we wanted to—no one on the planet is that creative.

The secular left is an amalgam of mayhem, a veritable Star Wars bar scene, a rogue gallery of freaks, geeks, nuts, sluts, slick politcos and skanky hos—and we're letting them walk without skewering the living daylights out of them.

What's wrong with us? We've become nicer than Christ.

From Hollywood to the Hill, the Left and those who lean that way do more psychotic stuff than my one-eyed uncle Joe does on a three day weekend binge when he's all liquored up. They are a MadTV, SNL and HBO Special waiting to happen. There has to be some conservative capital lying around that can be earmarked to gather no-holds-barred comedians to paper shred these little darlings on TV and in film. So why don't conservatives crank out comedians? Here's why I think our comedic contributions are weak:

1. Conservatives, obviously, don't think comedy is important. The Daily Show and The Colbert Report don't have The Factor numbers. Thus, they don't seem to be as important as O'Reilly, or Rush or Hannity in an immediate sense. And they're not. However, Steve and John do have the ear of millions of 18-35 year olds, who will, uh . . . hello, be at the wheel driving this nation a few short years from now. That's kinda significant.

The Right is foolish and stupid to not be knocking themselves out to compete for the belly laughs of this demographic. Blowing off this bunch that's not listening to conservative talk radio, watching Bill, or logging on to TownHall.com is to diss a crowd that will, in short order, be influencing our nation after you take the big dirt nap, conservative mom and dad.

Conservatives have got to get their ideas to the masses in modes other than talk radio, online newsportals, and Fox News. If conservs want to do more than choir preach and want to get their message to the young masses, then comedy and satire must come to the forefront.

2. We spit out lame comedians. When it comes to conservatives and Christians doing comedy, like soup in a bad restaurant, their brains are better left unstirred. Conservative comedians, especially Christian comedians, are not that funny. The reason why? Well, I think they're too nice. They don't really set the hook. They don't really deliver the dig. For some reason, the laughmeisters of the Right are PC addled. Fear of negative press has gripped most of our funny men and women. When one is worried about what others will think they cannot really queue up to deliver a scorching and hilarious screed aimed at deflating whoever they're after. Political correctness kills the comedian's ability to say what needs to be said and how they need to say it. If conservatives want to compete comically they're going to have to get raw. I'm talkin' gloves off UCF slugfest funny.

3. We're too serious. With our War with whacked out Islam and our ideological battle with the Secularists who whiz on traditional American values, the conservative can become a sober and somber person, which is understandable.

That doesn't mean we can't laugh, or more specifically, mock our enemies. Satire, comedy and laughter are great stress relievers and confidence builders. It's a show of strength. It's a sign that you're ready to play. Nowadays, we won't dare do cartoons about Osama and his ilk lest we tick them off. Are you kidding me? We're trying to kill the terrorists, right? Let me see if I get this correct: We can kill them, but we can't insult them with cartoons or sitcoms?

In regards to the secularists and their jacked up notions of where they'd like to take America, when the killer conservative comedians come forth and deftly employ their craft, I believe they will sway, through laughter, tens of thousands of ideological fence straddlers who are just waiting for us to get more hip and lighten up a bit.

Comedy is a tool the conservatives have to champion and use against the secularists tools on the left. Look, it's not enough to just sit back and moan about the things we don't like. We've got to go the extra mile and have fun at their expense . . . all the while tabling, in an entertaining way, what we believe will uphold this great land and that for which it stands.

One of the reasons why some young people no likey conservatives is because no one is making them look at the Left and then laugh their butts off at them. It seems shallow, but that's reality. I believe we need to change this by going Monty Python nuts. I'm willing to give it a try. My wife says I'm pretty funny, especially during sex. I'm not quite sure what she means, though.

Chapter 35.

Olbermann's Obsession with O'Reilly

My wife and I had a friend over for dinner the other night. After enjoying a tender backstrap off an axis deer I shot in Texas last year with my Ruger #1 chambered for the antiquated .275 Rigby round, mi amigo and I plopped our middle-aged butts down in the living room and switched on the tube.

We each fired up a big fat stogie (long ashes and big butts boys!) and sipped some Johnny Walker Blue as I blew through the various channels trying to find a show that sucked the least. Finding nothing but idiots aplenty, I went into default mode and switched on Fox News to see whose skull O'Reilly was crushing that night.

It was standard Bill fare: ball busting child molesters, cranking on cultural coarsening miscreants, interpreting the physical ticks of Britney with the body language lady, and shouting up the troops in Iraq as he augured a return to traditional American values.

As we watch O'Reilly war on sordid fellows of the baser sort, my buddy Oscar Sastoque of the Miami Fitness Connection turned and asked me if I had watched Keith Olbermann lately on MSNBC.

After retrieving my cigar I had spit across the room and cleaning up the whiskey I'd reflexively thrown over my shoulder when queried, I said, "No. I'm an American. And if you have, you can leave my house now." Oscar calmed me down, assuring me that he hadn't gone over to the dark side, and said that Keith had gone off-kilter with his O'Reilly "must die" fixation.

I figured, what the heck, I'll check it out. Surely God wouldn't send me to hell for watching a little MSNBC would he? Sure, he might put under a minor negative sanction for wasting my time or not using my mind properly, but hell? Nah. He probably would let it slide, seeing how my job is to remain aware of what the loopy left is doing. So, I took a long draw on the puros and a biting sip of Johnny's best and turned over to Keith to see if he was unraveling like Oscar said he was.

I couldn't believe what I saw and heard. Keith was going ballistic, obsessing about O'Reilly like a jealous and rabid Jan Brady drowning in her sister Marsha's praise wake. To me it wasn't as offensive as it was pathetic—and pathetic it was.

Y'know . . . envy isn't pretty. You and I both know that this is what Keith's Salieri-like preoccupation with Bill is all about, namely ugly and uncut China white envy. MSNBC's ratings are dragging like a fat man in a marathon, so instead of re-tooling and figuring out why they blow, the wizards at MSNBC decided to fuel Keith's jealous wrath.

Envy is a nasty sin. We don't hear about envy much because it's not that sexy, and in our totemic view of vice it doesn't get the lion's share of attention, but it is a deadly sin. Envy is the one sin the sinner will never like or admit. The more envy grows, the more it drives its impenitent coddler insane.

So, what is envy? Let me take off my smart ass hat and put on my theological one. I'll start with what envy is not. It's not admiring what someone else has and wanting some good stuff also. It is good to crave. A man's appetite will make him work.

Where envy differs from admiration/emulation is that envy is "sorrow at another's good" (Thomas Aquinas). Someone who's centered can watch another person, or a party, or a nation righteously prosper and not hate them for it.

The petty, envious person sees someone else excel and is slapped in the face with the reality that he just got dogged. So, instead of sucking it up and working harder and smarter, the unwise, envious one allows his pride to fuel his wounded spirit. This sets the dejected perp down a path of disparagement of the prosperous that eventually morphs into the desire to destroy the person, party or nation that has just trumped him.

Os Guinness states that the sin of envy has several common characteristics:
1. Envy is the vice of proximity. We are always prone to envy people close to us in temperament, gifts or position.
2. Envy is highly subjective. It is in the eye of the beholder. It is not the objective difference between people that feeds envy, but the subjective perception. As a Russian proverb says, "envy looks at a juniper bush and sees a pine forest."
3. Envy doesn't lessen with age. It gets worse as we run into more and more people with happiness and success, offering more fodder for envy.
4. Envy is often petty but always insatiable and all-consuming. However small the occasion that gives rise to it, envy becomes central to the envier's whole being. The envier "stews in his juice." Envy begins with pride and then plunges the person into hatred.
5. Envy is always self-destructive. What the envier cannot enjoy, no one should enjoy, and thus the envier loses every enjoyment. The envier's motto is

"if not I, then no one." As an eighth-century Jewish teacher put it, "the one who envies gains nothing for himself and deprives the one he envies of nothing. He only loses thereby."

Y'know, of all the stuff a person in Olbermann's position could righteously go after, he chooses rather to use his time to take O'Reilly down. But this is what the left is now all about: character assassination. They don't have answers, they don't have the ratings, they don't have the ear of the working hard, playing hard, God-loving, flag-saluting American public, so instead of waking the hell up they have decided to run with their foolhardiness and do it in prime time. Pretty sad gents, pretty sad.

Chapter 36.

Larry Craig is not Gay—
He Has Restless Crotch Syndrome

As all of you know by now, Idaho Senator Larry Craig was busted several weeks ago for attempting to get his summer groove on with a Minnesota Serpico in a Minneapolis airport toilet. Yes, it appears that Larry tried to get a party started by playing footsie with an undercover cop who was trying to offload a chimichanga he just had for lunch.

I guess Justin Timberlake isn't the only one trying to bring sexy back.

I have a question for the homosexual community: Is this a normal gay thing . . . the . . . uh . . . toilet sex? Help me out, those in the know, are the urges that crazy and intense? Can't they just wait until they get back to their Miata or a Motel 6 and resist the urge to do the funky monkey in a nasty public lavatory?

Hasn't the gay community watched Seinfeld and (with the rest of us) become germaphobes? I thought that you guys were, on the whole, persnickety and would be too fastidious to seek fulfillment in a stinking john. However, I just remembered that one of your sources of inspiration is George Michael so . . . never mind.

You know, as much as this situation sucks for Craig, he had better thank God that he hit on a cop and not a redneck.

If someone tried to rub my foot and give me elaborate Boy George hand signals while I'm bilging in the stall next door, I would:
- A). crush his metatarsals like Queen Latifah on a live cockroach,
- B). drain my bladder in the shoe housing his newly-crushed foot,
- C). proceed to stuff his balding head in the toilet he was using, and . . .
- D). call the cops to haul his near-drowned, lesson-learned, badly-beaten body to the nearest police department.

The thing that slays me is that after Craig said "I'm guilty" of harassing a cop with complex foot and hand signals like some nutty, gay third base coach trying to wave a runner in, he did a 180 and said "I'm not guilty" and "I'm not gay." In addition, he stated during his freak-out press conference this week that Scarlett Johansson is not hot, Woody Allen has great hair, and that he was the real fifth Beatle.

Look, Larry, none of us are buying the not guilty and not gay claims. If you want the GP to believe your nonsense, what you need to do is invent some malady to blame for your behavior. Our dysfunctional and therapeutic community will buy that horse crap, and I guarantee that a drug company will create a pill for your fabricated pain.

Howzabout something like this: You're a victim of RCS (Restless Crotch Syndrome). That's it! Think about it. You have an illness that made you try to crawl into another guy's stall. Are you smelling what I'm cooking? It's not your fault; you never would have violated the cop's space if you had had some Horndoginex. Whew! What a weight off your shoulders! You owe me money for that one, LC.

Seriously folks, why can't anyone just say that they're guilty and deserve whatever whipping comes their way when they're caught red-handed doing stupid, stupid stuff? I know every sinful and dumb thing that I have done, regardless of the extenuating circumstances, has ultimately been my fault, except for the other day when a really slow driver was making me late for an appointment and caused me to blow through a red light onto the sidewalk and crush seven cats. That was grandma's fault officer, not mine.

Whatever happened to good old-fashioned "I suck, please forgive me God" repentance? Listen to me Larry: Don't be an OJ; he's a pariah who will live on in infamy. Be thou the penitent one and own whatever you have done, dude.

To heck with public opinion and what people will think. Focus rather on the inevitable mano-a-mano that you will one day have with God (and He can't be buffaloed). Let that pending appointment guide thee to get real with yourself, your family, and the public. Sure you might lose face with some folks (you already have), and yes your career will, ironically, go down the toilet (it already has), but at least you will have a clean conscience before God and some public respect for owning it when you have blown it.

Chapter 37.

Our Honorable Hunters and the Pain-in-the-Butt Tree Huggers

Regnery Publishing is about to further bury the loons on the Left with its latest installment in the Politically Incorrect Guide series. Who's in the crosshairs this time in this destined to be best-selling tome, you ask? Well, honey, it is the frothy and paranormal twinkies on the left who hate hunting and hunters and spread lies about us and the important role hunting plays within the world we live.

Author Frank Miniter, executive editor of American Hunter magazine, is the lucky duck who Regnery chose for the fun job of intellectually thrashing the lying liberals who whiz on our great sport and the vital role it plays in all of our lives.

Frank had to be chuckling with crazy glee as he banged away on his laptop, not just writing his personal opinions or wet-eyed, Disney-fueled feelings but rather the cold, hard, positive and objective empirical data about the truly excellent things that hunters bring—literally—to the table.

Here's a tiny list, a mere smattering of blistering and irrefutable particulars you will find in the *Politically Incorrect Guide to Hunting* that hunters provide for animals and people, stuff like:

- Hunters donate tons of meat to food pantries, pay the fees that expand wildlife conservation programs,

keep national parks preserved, and protect motorists' lives.
- Hunters are true nature lovers and conservationists and are the first to report poachers who disregard laws that protect wildlife and natural habitats.
- Hunter-funded conservation groups are primarily responsible for bringing back American wildlife that was nearly extinct in the last century.
- Hunting is safer than soccer, football, baseball, cheerleading and ping pong.
- California game managers must wait 'til a cougar threatens a human before they can rock its world. How sweet. Because of this brain fart, today the number of people that naughty cougars have killed has doubled from what it was before cougar hunting was banned.
- Deer kill ten times the number of people as sharks, cougars, bears and alligators combined, as well as more than commercial airline, bus and train accidents combined.
- When the greenies protected the alligators on Sanibel Island, Florida, the alligators ate the tree huggers and their dogs!
- Bear attacks are at an historic high, and you're more likely to be attacked by a bear where hunting isn't allowed—like in a national park.
- Bears with no fear of humans often attack after hearing gunshots—a dinner bell that a deer or elk is waiting for them—and thanks to the tree huggers, hunters can't do anything about it.
- Aviation collisions with wildlife cost $500 million annually.
- Livestock losses to predators cost $71 million annually.

- Hunting protects trees from being destroyed by scavenging deer. Those trees help protect land from erosion and house songbird populations.
- Vegetarians who don't eat meat because they love animals are eating vegetables from farmers who kill deer, rabbits and vermin that would destroy the vegans' lunch. Remember that, hypocrites, when you crunch your little baby carrots and worship your edamame beans.

As stated above, this is just a simple sampling of the stonking truths Frank pummels the pro-stupidity anti-hunting cabal with.

However, I don't expect this book to convert the implacable, closed-to-reality PETA types. Nothing can. They're gonzo. What this book will do, though, is provide the hunter and the hunter-friendly person with intellectual fodder to defend this primal and noble sport and significant specifics of why hunting is a must for mankind.

Hunters, you will feel proud and unashamed after you plow through this preponderance of evidence which paints you in the good light you should be painted in. Every hunter should get this pro-hunting compendium, read it, and then declare its contents loud and proud.

Now, let's see . . . next weekend I've got a wild boar hunt. Yes, it seems that Porky Pig is destroying the tomatoes you vegans love to eat on my buddy's 7,000 acre south Florida farm. We will shoot as many as we can for you . . . the vegetarian.

What else? Oh yeah, in November I'm going with my daughter to my friend's ranch in Texas, and we'll take an assortment of native and exotic game. In January I'll be gator hunting in the wild swamps of the everglades, and then in June it's back to Africa to hunt the cradle's mighty critters.

Just with these hunts alone, I will put into circulation mucho money which will go to conservation, not to mention that my friends and I will feed hundreds of needy people low fat, high protein yummy meat. What about you, tree humper? How much money will you spend for conservation, and how much food will you provide for the poor in the next few months? I guarantee whatever it is, it doesn't come remotely close to what the true animal and nature lovers, the hunters, provide.

Chapter 38.

Rosie and Khalid Sittin' in a Tree . . . K-I-S-S-I-N-G
(Written March 17th, 2007)

Khalid Sheikh Mohammed (KSM) painted himself during his trial this week at Club Gitmo as employee of the decade for Al Qaeda's Death Monkey Squad. This piece of Samsonite prattled on with Islamic glee about his noxious brain farts such as . . .

- The suicide hijackings of 9/11. Remember 9/11/2001? Think back, way back to like . . . uh . . . 5 ½ years ago when 3,000 people died during a terrorist attack here on U.S. soil. Does that ring a bell? It doesn't? Just google it. It was pretty bad.
- Personally cutting off Danny Pearl's head.
- The Bali night club bombings which blew to smithereens a couple of hundred people.
- The killing of one U.S. Marine on an island off Kuwait.
- The 2002 bombing of a Kenya beach resort frequented by Israelis.
- The failed missile attack on an Israeli passenger jet after it took off from Mombasa, Kenya.

And if that wasn't industrious enough, KSM (according to himself) had many other things up his long sleeve dress. Stuff like: plans to off a couple of U.S. Presidents (Carter and Clinton . . . Go figure!), rub out Pope John Paul II and Pakistan's President Musharaf, plus bring down the Sears Tower in Chi Town. Uh . . . let's see . . . what else? Oh yeah, bomb the Empire State Building, the New York Stock Exchange, the Panama Canal, some big clock in London and Heathrow Airport.

All in all, this one Muslim has claimed responsibility for masterminding the deaths of several thousand people and had tens of thousands of others marked for mayhem had not Bush and his boys busted the bastard.

But then again, this all could be a scam cooked up by the Bush administration. Yes! That's it! It's all lies. Lies, I tell you. That is, if I am to believe Rosie O'Donnell (what a waste of an apostrophe!). According to Orca, I mean, Facts-Be-Damned-O'Donnell, Khalid Sheikh Mohammed is a mere kitty cat, and that mean old Bush has Lee Harvey'd him. Khalid wasn't involved in any of the above. C'mon people. Wake up. That was Osama and Osama alone. We're being hoodwinked and bamboozled by Bush, dammit, at least according to Rosie's sweaty vociferations on The View.

The reason the shabby Sheikh confessed to these atrocities, thus saith the Rose, was because he was tortured. O'Donnell points to such evidence of his suffering to things like KSM's ugly Glamour photo.

Yes, according to Mama Cass, for three years the CIA has been messing up Khalid's hair (probably a series of violent noogies), not allowing him to shave very often and making him wear a Flash Dance T-shirt—and that lethal combination eventually caused the boy to cave. He couldn't take it, man. He got to the place where he'd own anything for some Brylcreem, a Trac2 and some lycra.

Rosie and Khalid Sittin' in a Tree . . . K-I-S-S-I-N-G

Rosie bellowed, on the show she has now Jezebelled, that KSM is not an animal, but a man. I've got some news for you Rosie: so are you. As a matter of fact, take a picture of O'Donnell . . . any picture . . . and scribble a mustache on her/it, then scratch in some 5 0'clock shadow on her jowls and poof . . . you got yourself a Khalid Sheikh Mohammed! Try it. It's fun. That's why I think the big Rose is going to bat so hard for Khalid; They have so much in common, both physically and ideologically.

Barbara Walters, if you read my column (and I know you do, baby love . . . and sorry for not returning your calls yesterday), listen to me: You've got to fire Rosie now. Don't be afraid of her. The veterinarians at the New York City Zoo have tranquilizer darts that'll knock her straight out so that you can have her air lifted out of the building. It'll be okay.

Babs, the girl is certifiable. Not only because she's of the genus bovinae, but also because the girl has gone crazy! Do America a favor: get a saner chick on your show. Or get a good looking crazy girl. Or—if you're going to do crazy, then get Charlie Manson. Channel him in every day from Corcoran State Prison and let's watch him swing from a sprinkler pipe in his cell and howl at the moon. Chuck's got two things on Rosie: 1) He's more creative with his conspiracy theories and 2) He's a better looking woman. Just a thought . . . toss it around with your producers and Joy and Elizabeth. Conference me in if you need to.

Lastly, in light of the Sheikh's confession, I propose the following:
1. I say we give Bush and his crew a much deserved standing ovation for getting KSM.
2. Next, I say we "rob" Khalid of his humanity. He robbed us. We rob him. I suggest we strip him of his humanity with a bullet and broadcast it on Pay-Per-View.

3. On second thought, we shouldn't kill him. Then he'd be praised as a martyr. Let's keep him alive.
4. Instead of killing him, let's put him in a non-air-conditioned cell down here in Miami, feed him ham sandwiches, only to be chased down with skunk urine while playing a 24/7/365 loop of Boy George's music video "Do You Really Wanna Hurt Me?" with the volume ratcheted way up in his cell that's been wallpapered, floor to ceiling, with O'Donnell in a Brazilian bikini. Let him experience a little temporal hell before he goes to an eternal one.
5. Whaddya think, too harsh? Yeah, it reads too harsh.
6. Let's just shoot the guy and be done with him. No use torturing him.
7. Stay sober. Even though KSM was a major kernel of corn in the turd which is militant Islam, we can't obsess on him now as there are thousands of murderous others currently looking to fill his sandals, and we've got to keep busy capturing and killing them.

Chapter 39.

Satan Takes a Little Nap After Dr. D. James Kennedy Passes Away
(Written September 8th, 2007)

This week the church lost one of its great generals, Dr. D. James Kennedy. Kennedy, senior Pastor of Coral Ridge Presbyterian Church, chancellor of Knox Theological Seminary, founder of Evangelism Explosion (and a stack of other ministries), made Satan more frustrated than Ted Nugent would be watching Dianne Feinstein attempt to shatter the Guinness Book of World Records' longest break dance.

Yes, Dr. Kennedy was a disaster to El Diablo and his defeated ilk.

Having been a student of Knox Theological Seminary, I had the honor of meeting Kennedy on several occasions and listening to him preach at his church and teach in our classes. He / KTS even bought a massive (and beautiful, I might add) painting I did of John Knox which hangs in the seminary today.

Being the sardonic skeptic that I am, I'm not easily impressed by ministers nowadays. I am especially jaded toward the megachurches that are run by the super-coifed, Colgate-grinning, Rembrandt veneer type of guys. Most of these boys are preening narcissists, snake oil opportunists par excellence who are in the ministry simply because they can't be Bon Jovi. Kennedy, on the other hand, impressed me. He was an old school reformer of a different stripe.

Here are two things I liked about Dr. D. James Kennedy:

1. He was driven by the Great Commission and the cultural mandate. Kennedy kept his sights locked on what Scripture tells Christians to focus on, namely the saving of souls and changing culture.

Most postmodern pastors don't do either anymore. Why don't they preach the gospel Kennedy style, you ask? Well Spanky, it is offensive and most ministers, with their ragged little egos, would rather be liked than right, so they dilute the message and thus delude the masses with something other than that which Christ and the apostles preached. Kennedy didn't do this. He was God's UPS man; he simply and faithfully delivered the package he was given: the gospel uncut, which is the power of God to transform people and nations.

Speaking of nations, Dr. K loved the U.S.A. and that for which it stands (or I guess used to stand for). This love for our God-kissed country caused him to fight to uphold its original Judeo-Christian roots and the continuity of our religious liberties.

Jim Kennedy didn't buy the notion that Christians shouldn't be involved in influencing local, state and federal government, or the arts, or the educational system or anything else that goes down on God's green earth. And no, he wasn't a theocrat or a Christianist (whatever that is. Just make it up as you go, Lefties).

Yes, DJK believed that Christians should have a voice, a vote, and a right to speak up and out regarding what happens from Hollywood to Washington D.C. just as much as any freak group on the left does.

However, preachers of late have been cowed away from influencing culture for several reasons. Two indictments will suffice for now: 1. cultural influence demands hard work and, 2. it brings persecution.

Presently we have way too many ministers who are lazy and thin-skinned. Yes, they'd rather just let society go to hell rather than get off their glutes, dust off their brains and Bibles and get into the fray to stand for what's right and forever refuse to sit in the back of the secularists' bus. That's too painful. Yep, forget that. Going to Night of Joy in Orlando is much, much easier and so much fun! Pass the cotton candy.

2. He believed that sound doctrine matters. Doctrine was important to the good doctor. Kennedy appreciated the ministerial duty of dishing out the apostolic goods and believed that Christianity isn't a make it up as you go, whatever the cattle want, thang. Dr. Kennedy understood that the truths of the gospel were to be deeply understood, powerfully proclaimed and conscientiously preserved even if it was unpopular at the time. And this he did.

Contrast that with ministers today who place little or no value on sound doctrine because in our milieu it is all about feelings . . . nothing more than feelings. Oprah carries more weight with these cultural capitulators than Obadiah does, and you can bet your tithe check I'm right. Check it out. I'll bet you a lot of ministers are reading Donald Trump, Jack Welch and Tony Robbins more than they are Augustine, Luther or Calvin, as those guys are just so . . . so, like . . . yesterday. Kennedy, on the other hand, deeply imbibed Scripture and the writings of the greats of the church. Also (and this is weird) Dr. Kennedy actually earned his doctorate. Y'know, as in he went to grad school, studied and wrote a bunch of papers and stuff. Freak out, right?

Yes, in an age of flighty gimmick-laden Christian loosey-goosey-heretical-can't-scrape-this-stuff-off-your-shoe religious schlock, Jim Kennedy was *semper fidelis* to Christ and the eternal gospel.

I have to admit that I am sad with Kennedy's passing. I'm sad not because Kennedy passed away, since he's in heaven now straight tripping having his mind blown like none of us can even imagine. The thing that makes me sad is that Kennedy's absence represents a loss in a near-extinct breed of preachers who can truly throw a weighty temporal and eternal spiritual punch.

Thankfully at Knox Seminary, the torch has been successfully passed to their profs and to the hundreds of young men who have graduated from its hallowed halls. So I guess I'm not that sad because the DNA, though scarce, is still alive.

Matter of fact, boys contemplating ministry, if you feel called to God's service why don't you blow off that easy, greasy, cheesy school you picked out and have KTS rake you over their coals? It will be hard. They won't allow you to skate. And they won't give you "life credit," little darling, but they will equip you to reach the lost and shake this nation for the glory of God.

Y'know, when I think of Kennedy and the righteous legacy he left for God and Country, for some bizarre reason (probably because I am bizarre), I call to mind an interview I saw with Nikki Sixx, the former bass player for Motley Crüe. The interviewer asked Sixx what his band's "goals" were, of which Nikki replied, "I wanna leave a scar on the planet."

Dr. Kennedy left a scar. Not an unrighteous one, as Sixx hoped to leave, but a scar nonetheless. Yep, I believe Dr. D. James Kennedy left a searing and sizable blemish on Satan's sagging and haggard backside.

Chapter 40.

Help! I'm Being Nifonged!

If I were Mike Nifong's son or daughter, I'd change my last name PDQ. Why? Well, principally because that name has now formally become a pejorative in the American argot for anyone who will gleefully roast the innocent for their pipe dream of power.

Y'know, it's just a matter of time before FOX has a new reality show championing the cause of folks who've been trampled by such soulless narcissists. The show could be called, "Help! I'm being Nifonged!"

Blinded by ambition in his quest to be Durham's DA, Democrat Mike Nifong (why didn't you listen to your mother when she told you, "If you don't stop you'll go blind!") has officially become the biggest DA in the US.

There are several other ding dongs aside from Nifong whom we ought to continue to give a real rough time for being complicit in the Nifonging of the Duke Lacrosse players. People like the local cop who gave oversight to this Circus Stupidus who is notorious for his disdain for Duke students. I think his name is . . . Sgt. Gollieb.

Then you've got the shriveled testicle Board of (mis)Trustees and the admin cats at Duke who, cowed by what people might think of them, decided to serve these boys to the lions—facts be damned.

Let's see . . . who else do we have that we must hound, disdain and then ignore forever? Of course, what is wrong with me? I must be getting old. I almost forgot the three race baiting stooges: namely, Al Sharpton, Jesse Jackson and the what's-his-name Black Panther Party Leader. When are these screaming ninnies going to come forth and apologize for being ridiculously wrong on this issue and for wasting our time with their vile vomit via TV?

And lastly, we have the village bicycle . . . the person who put this ball in play . . . you know who I'm talking about: Crystal Gail Mangum, the black stripper who jumped on the let's-bash-and-make-some-cash-off-the-educated-well-off-white-guy band wagon. Thanks, girlfriend, for screwing up so many lives with your stupid, vicious lies. Have a good life.

I bet these wrongfully accused and publicly deep-fried boys are currently breathing subterranean sighs of relief while at the same time enjoying a big piece of shadenfreude pie at Nifong's expense. Eat it up boys. You deserve it!

Yep, I guarantee the cold beers that Collin, Reade, David, their girlfriends and their parents are sipping on have never tasted sweeter as they now watch Nifong swing, like Haman, on the gallows of public scorn he initially erected for them.

I'm not God, but if I were, not only would my new book become a bestseller, but I would also make sure of these two things: first, that I got to go elephant hunting with my good buddy Glenn Kendall in Tanzania this fall and second, that there is a special place . . . a little eternal corner in hell . . . complete with a huge dunce cap for an impenitent guy like Nifong who came so close to making these boys' temporal lives a complete and utter living hell.

Amen.

Chapter 41.

Christ the Contrarian

When Jesus Christ got injected into the human mix two thousand plus years ago, from the cradle to the cross, He was a lightning rod of controversy. His incarnation heated up the culture war more than O'Reilly could ever dream of doing.

Immanuel's arrival upon the scene caused-demon inspired political idiots to try to kill Him while He was still cooing and pooing in His pampers. The dragon no likey his party getting ruined, and ruin it the Prince of Peace did.

The initial message the Wonderful Counselor preached, according to Dr. Luke's take, ticked off the crowd He was addressing so thoroughly that they attempted to throw Him off a cliff. He nailed that haughty mob for the crud they were practicing—and He did so publicly. In public. Ouch. Snap! That's not very "Christian" of Christ.

In reality (on this planet), Jesus received minimal accolades. No lucrative gigs with the Premier Speakers Bureau; no "isn't He so nice let's put Him on Oprah" invite; no fat, Creflo Dollar like honorariums; no limousine chariot services. He got nada, nothing, zilch, zero, zippo—and for those who haven't seen The Passion of the Christ yet, it sorta got even rougher.

Today in our radically wussified, politically correct state of bland, we won't embrace this Christ because He'd so get under our skin. And we like our skin. The truth of the matter is that what Jesus said and did caused more discomfort to man's me-monkey human spirit than cheap Tequila and three bags of pork rinds drenched in hot sauce would to Martha Stewart's colon (insert deep belch and loud fart noise here).

It's funny that a bunch of churchgoers who worship Jesus probably wouldn't hire Him to be their pastor today because He was too much of a hellrazer. His solid/acidic, anti-bovine scatology posture toward politicians, priests, pet sins, oppressors and others who were playing games with God and man equates to a résumé that most pastoral search committees wouldn't touch with a ten foot pew.

Y'know, most of us forget the above when we see sweet baby Jesus lying in a manger. Because of our rank illiteracy regarding Scripture, our prejudiced and politically correct approach to the Bible that's custom-tailored a Jesus of our own imaginations, we have developed a deep distaste for anything but a bespoke and neutered little "g" god.

My prayer for you and yours, our churches and our nation is that we flush the feckless, Lysol-disinfected, feminine hygiene Jesus we've created to mollycoddle our madness and go back to the rowdy Christ who would, lovingly of course, shake us into shape.

So, as we're clicking our mouse and melting our plastic this holiday season in homage to the birth of heaven's Beowulf, why don't we go the second mile and follow His example by being more rowdy for righteous stuff in '07. Yeah, that's it. Make 2007 one where the clash aspects of Christ's nature are emphasized. Possibly, by so doing, we will see personal sin, aggressive secularism and militant Islam get staved off like never before.

Have a merry contrarian Christmas and a happy, hell-razing New Year.

Chapter 42.

Our Shrinkage in the Global War on Terror

Bill O'Reilly stated this week on "The Factor" (Tuesday, 12/5/06) that the West is failing to confront evil. Failing to confront evil? Heck, we're scared to define it, much less take it head-on.

We won't even draw cartoons regarding this enemy, lest we offend our killers. Wow! Murderous Muslims all over the world must be making girlie man, wussy, limp wrist jokes about the West, as they bounce their combies down whatever dirt road they're on en route to secure a nuke (or two) with our name on it.

The failure to define what is "evil" is causing us to capitulate to the apex (or nadir, I guess) of political correctness in a "no %$@&" time of crisis. Go ahead; ask someone at the next Winter Solstice office party to define "evil." You'll get the typical "it's all relative" slop, or "there is no objective standard of right or wrong," or "all absolute truth claims are nothing more than powerplays, man." Y'know, the same emblematic drivel your pot smoking, liberal prof taught you at the University of You-Just-Wasted-A-Ton-Of-Your-Parent's- Cash-And-Got-Brain-Washed-In-The-Process.

The few who do have the cojones to say something is evil will be called evil themselves because judging something as wrong has become the sin of the 21st century—unless, of course, you're a liberal; then you can judge, bring up Foley, Delay, Ted Haggard, other GOP inadequacies, evangelical inconsistencies and call a spade a shovel all you want.

Anyway, postmodernism, as Os Guinness says, has made it "worse to judge evil than to do evil." Those who declare something to be damnable are evil themselves, at least according to grand wizards of secular progressive "thought."

In addition to the West's growing unwillingness to say the Islamofascist ideology is uncut crap to the third power and that their adherents need to be deleted like KFed's website history, here are three more reasons why I think the West's will to war has shrunk:

1. We couldn't care less. We don't want to be bothered with what's going on with the war on Iraq or with other mean people. We don't want to stay abreast about what militant Islam is up to these days. That's complicated, depressing and just icky. No, our inquiring minds want to know the following: What's up with Britney and her un-photogenic crotch? Is Brit gonna be OK? How come Jen and Vince broke up? Did Mischa Barton have a meltdown? What's Nicole Ritchie's plastic surgery secret behind her new sexy look? Why did Kidman put new hubby Keith on a short leash? Is a Nip/Tuck star really leaving the show? And what's up with the Martha and Rachel Ray food fight?

2. We want to believe the spin coming from CAIR (The Council on American-Islamic Relations) because the truth about Muslim mayhem is too brutal. Because of our aversion to the rawness of what the West is really facing with militant Islam, we want to believe CAIR's talking heads when they say that "everything is cool, and the radicals in the Islamic camp are few and far between." The reality is that the danger we face is higher, deeper, wider and nearer than most of us would care to understand. Since reality bites and requires

that we change, we'd just rather believe the fairy tales about our enemies from their propaganda/reality stylists. As far as I'm concerned, CAIR is to prevarication what Carrot Top is to red hair coloring, tie dyed T-Shirts, over exercising and unfunniness.

3. We think we can talk our way out of this mess. We believe we can Eddie Haskell militant Islam and bebop and scat our way out of their ill will. The only problem is that Islam is not some June Cleaver that can be manipulated by our impish charm. We are convinced that we can solve things with Iran and Syria with a little less talk and a little more conversation. Yes, the PoMo wannabe placaters of the implacable would like to sit down with Islamofascists (who will never help us, ever loathe us, and forever seek to kill us) and tell them that "You're not evil; you simply have a hole in your soul that we would like to help you fill. We should not be fighting. Can't we all get along? We should talk more often . . . maybe get together, play some checkers . . . and we'd love to have you over for dessert to eat a piece of strawberry pie."

Militant Islam has got to be loving the indecision, division and erosion of the West's will to war. They understand the ancient maxim that a kingdom divided against itself cannot stand. We're increasingly becoming so divided and defeated that if we don't watch it, as one comedian said, we could be approaching a long, drawn-out debate regarding which shade of white to use as our surrender flag.

I believe we can be united and that we will eventually wake up and deal with radical Islam; however, I also believe (and fear) that the cohesion, readiness and resolve we need now to truly hammer these death dealers will only come about after we get hammered once again. I'm talking 911-style or worse. And I'm thinking this will probably occur in the next one to three years. And I hope I'm wrong.

Chapter 43.

Obama Wants Your Evangelical Mama's Vote

Barack Obama is to Christianity what Michael Jackson is to heterosexuality. He might be one, but he's not the poster child for the cause. You know, when I watch Obama and the other overtly ideological southpaws queue up to play the Christ card, it takes me back to Kerry in '04 when he tried to convince gun owners and hunters that he was a Nimrod.

The fact is that if evangelicals didn't represent a president-making voting block, they would get the same attention from our liberal brethren as Linda Tripp at a *Playboy* party. Since evangelicals swing a big stick, the Democrats (who have been rabidly anti-religious in their rhetoric up until, uh . . . today) have begun to stamp dove and fish stickers on their bids for office, and Barack is leading their haggard Hallelujah chorus.

Yeah, as of late, Obama has been telling his compadres that they need to cease and desist with the anti-Christ blather and dial down when it comes to:

1. dissing the role faith plays in the American collective,
2. going Rosie whenever "God" or "Christ" or "Moses" is mentioned in public,

3. trying to butcher the Pledge of Allegiance because it contains the phrase "under God" and because of their fear that "it could, if repeated often enough, morph a child into Jerry Falwell—slick hair, big belly, Bible and all."

This is cool, and I appreciate BO throwing us conservative Bible-thumpers a bone in trying to relax his party's violent knee jerks to our religious liberties; however, the aforementioned props that Barack is currently (and possibly temporarily) parsing out are really no consolation when it comes to the strident, anti-biblical views this young hopeful holds. Y'know, like the stuff my colleague Kevin McCullough recently pointed out:

1. As a state legislator he actively worked to preserve availability of abortion in all nine months of pregnancy.
2. He opposed parental notification for abortion.
3. He opposed any and all bans on partial birth abortion (an act that includes delivery of the baby up to the head, the crushing of the baby's brain, the suctioning of the brain matter and then completed delivery of the child's deflated cranium).
4. In his run for the U.S. Senate, Obama asked his wife to pen a letter to Illinois voters that reassured them of his commitment to fighting for the right to butcher children in the womb.
5. His long support of the advance of the radical homosexual activist lobby in their pursuit to destroy traditional marriage.
6. His support of the creation of "special rights" for people who engage in homosexuality for the sole purpose of putting them at the front of the line on issues of employment, housing and litigation.

7. His solid backing of the advancement of all "hate crimes" legislation, which ultimately may be used to silence clergy who believe, according to their own convictions, that homosexual behavior is wrong and preach the same from biblical texts.
8. His perfect voting record against the defense of marriage.
9. He advocates continued funding for Planned Parenthood clinics in our nation's inner cities, which are performing genocide against the populations of African Americans living there.
10. And most damnable of all, when a brave nurse named Jill Stanek brought about national awareness to a practice at a local hospital in suburban Chicago that allowed the starvation and neglect of newly born children who had survived abortion procedures, Obama—"the Christian"—opposed her. He opposed the rights of those children to be given the chance to live, and he advocated against a ban on such procedures—then known as "born alive abortions."

C'mon, Barack. You can't play the Mother-Teresa- I'm-a-good-Christian-man card when your voting record is that watery towards biblical verities. The only way Obama and his followers can keep Christ and their liberal credo is to blow off huge chunks of the Bible and replace the Scriptures with make-believe notions of postmodernism's new malleable "Christ."

The Christian skipping around the maypole wearing his rose-colored glasses who has a bent to the liberal left needs to understand something: If it were left up to the modern, secularized liberal establishment, they would be marginalized to a spiritual ghetto on the sidelines of life.

Your vote for a liberal "Christian" is most likely a vote for:

- Christianity to be scrubbed from government and whatever turf the government owns.
- Secularism to be continually mainlined into our public school system and for Christianity to be vilified in campus life.
- Public officials, employees and appointees to be pressured to hide their faith in the closet and suppress their public displays of belief in God lest they be grouped with Hitler or Osama and then fired.
- Public attacks on churches and Christians in a continued attempt to restrict them in the private sector.
- The continued media endorsement of the same putrid, hedonistic stuff that sunk ancient civilizations. You could then expect your kids to continue to be exposed to things that only Kid Rock sees backstage.
- Terrorists to move about and organize more freely.

Modern liberalism, no matter how Barack and his buddies prop up their Church of the New Groove, tosses out Scripture on several different and solemn levels. How a true believer in Christ (Christ as defined by the Bible) can say he or she believes in what Jesus, the prophets and apostles said *and* side with such a liberal politico simply because he is "positive and youthful" is beyond me.

Christian, don't over steer to the Left because the Right has driven parts of our party and nation into the ditch. I know portions of the GOP suck when it comes to standing up to biblical principles. However, we suck less than the liberals do.

One last thing, Barack Obama is Bill Clinton with a tan. Don't forget that.

Chapter 44.

Avoiding the Date from Hell

How does a girl avoid dating or marrying some festering bag of ripe compost like Kevin Federline and his helix-missing ilk? I know Britney Spears is about as sharp as a bag of wet mice; however, even with her low levels of discernment and her Turkish walnut-like density, I believe Brit (as well as those below and above her in brilliance) can, with a little guidance, steer relationally clear from any urge to merge with some future K-Fedian bad date.

So . . . how does a girl circumvent the date from hell? It's pretty simple, ladies. Follow the following principles, and you'll land yourself a quality catch. Blow them off, and you'll attract some Darwinian holdover who'll drain you emotionally, spiritually, physically and financially more than a hemi-powered robotic milker drains the dairy out of a cow.

Girlfriend, are you ready to leave in the dust some dude who's not worthy of sharing the air you breathe—much less your time and attention? You are? Well, giddy up! Here's the master list that will increase your chances of attracting a Prince Charming versus drawing some piece of Charmin.

Before you "get" a boyfriend . . .

Number One: Get a Life. A lot of ladies date disasters simply because they don't have squat going on in their own lives, and they think that the missing link is regularly French kissing the over-moussed bartender at Chili's. One way to make certain you do not get wrapped around the axle of the date from hell is to make sure you're kicking butt in life first—before you try to partner with anyone else.

Before you wade into the dating swamp, make sure you have something going on. Dissuade yourself right now from the debilitating notion that you need a man to be complete. Granted, great guys do add to the mix. That said, it's incumbent that you first have a life for a good man to add to.

A relationship with Dash Riprock is subservient to the priority that you are focused. Yeah, you need a vision more than you need a tripod. You need something great to live and die for first. You need to hear from God before you fuse to a fellow. If not, you'll be a gullible Etch-A-Sketch from some scribbling monkey.

Look ladies, if you enter into a relationship rudderless, like a needy parasite, you will become the slave of whatever host you hitched yourself to. You'll find yourself doing things . . . changing things . . . believing things . . . compromising things . . . and getting involved in crap you wouldn't even think of doing just because you neeeeeeeeeed him.

Girls get freaky when they don't have much going on in life. They try to over please, which is cool for two to three weeks for most guys, but then it gets a little nerve-gratingly old. Yes, the desire to please motivated from need can get whacked. It goes something like this: Girl -"Do you like my hair?" The guy pauses because he's watching a Bud Lite commercial. The co-dependant girl takes his pause as disapproval and spouts, "What—you don't like my hair? Is it my bangs? It's my bangs, isn't it? 'Cause I'll cut 'em. If you want me to, I'll cut my bangs. I swear to God, I'll cut 'em. Don't leave me! Arggh!"

Honeys, please, please, don't queue up to any person needing them to make you whole. Holy cow, señorita.

Looking to most guys nowadays for fulfillment, as one comedian said, is like looking to Michael Jackson for psychoanalysis. You've got to go to the desert. Get focused. You should have (again!) so much going on that if your guy dumps you like a chunk of concrete or if some dude doesn't like you it shouldn't cause a major hiccup in your life. Why? Well, you have a nation to save, a dragon to slay, a mountain to conquer, a mission to attend to, and it's that man's loss, not yours.

Listen, if a guy leaves you, or is not attracted to you, that shouldn't derail your existence. That shouldn't throw you into a neurotic never-ending introspective trip that leaves you depressed, jonesing on Bridget Jones, developing raccoon eyes from lack of sleep, or singing "I Can't Live if Living is Without You" while you gorge yourself on aerosol whipped cream.

Get a life (one more time) first, and you'll get a worthy man.

Number Two: Get a grip. The first thing to go when someone "feels" they're in love is all cognizant thought. Yeah, here's where the hormones forcefully kick logic's butt to the curb and begin to drive the girl's life like a drunk (or sober, for that matter) Gary Busey.

When the blood drains from the head to the crotch, men call this enjoyable but often-disastrous phenomenon thinking with their "little head." Though minus the particular member men are guilty of being partial to, girls can also make massive mistakes when their heads switch off and their "hearts" switch on.

Ladies, the key to keeping your pretty feet tethered to the planet when you roam out into the dating Serengeti is . . . (drum roll, please) . . . to think! God gave you a head, so use it. Get a grip. Try to stay sane, girlfriend, so that romance doesn't eclipse common sense.

If you find that you're having problems using your noggin, do these: First, keep your hands off each other 'til your brain catches up with your body. Second, don't blow off family and friends because they can help you see through the veil of crap that most bad guys hide behind.

Number Three: Get someone compatible. Paula Abdul said, "it ain't fiction it's a natural fact, we come together cuz opposites attract." And who are we to question the multiple divorced and serial bad dater, Paula Abduh? Girls, forget Miss Abdul's advice. Sure, opposites attract, but the real question is . . . will they stay intact when the poop hits the fan? And the answer is: highly unlikely.

Y'know, finding someone like-minded doesn't sound as sexy as dating the brooding, in and out of jail, melancholic, mysterious, exotic wannabe rebel flute player for the rock band Oasis who needs your breast to lie on in order for him to make sense out of life. Yes, ladies, if you'd like to have a successful relationship with longevity, you've got to blow off the Sugar Daddy, the Tommy Lee or the Olivier Martinez idol you're worshipping and realize that compatibility, not fantasy, is the key to the kingdom.

Number Four: Get Virtuous. Not letting the dillweed you just met hump your leg anytime soon is usually a sure-fire way to cudgel off the date from hell. This is no secret; the gibbering monkey that's inside a guy's pants wants inside of your pants, and he'll do anything to get it there, muy pronto. Yes, Pollyanna, men will lie, swear, pretend, go to church, walk backwards, watch Marie Antoinette or Nell, listen to Mariah Carey or Celine Dion, etc., just to unleash the beast.

However, ladies (if you haven't learned this yet, you will) once you let them in they are officially on their way out, and all you're left with is the icky thought that you actually had sex with the guy who drops fries at McDonald's. That's a horrible notion. Plus, there's about a 25% chance that you now have the gift that keeps on giving, an STD. Yippee!

Look ladies, reality is that sex with most guys is as about as eventful as an October Fest in downtown Miami. Don't believe me? Then ask some of your violated girlfriends after they've had a couple of beers. They'll confirm it. Being virtuous and guarding your garden 'til you get a worthy dude to put a ring on your finger saves you from the BS of possibly getting saddled with an STD, or becoming pregnant, or having your soul shattered like an ostrich egg shipped FedEx overnight when the guy finally dumps you for your room mate. Save it 'til you get married, girls, because a guy who'll wait that long is either gay or he really, really respects you. Hopefully, it's the latter.

Number Five: Get Solid Boundaries. Another great way to avoid dating some yard ape is to erect massive boundaries around your life. Have who you are and what you'll tolerate so solidly defined that all goofy guys can read it and weep.

You've got to stay guarded, girls. Let the guys call you stubborn, selfish, holier-than-thou, unfeeling, unyielding, unbeholden and unloving when you stay in your values corner. At least there won't be some porn video of you and him floating around on the internet for your grandparents to have emailed to them via YouTube, eh? With '60 ft. tall razor wire metaphysical prison fencing placed around you, you will assure that all suitors will respect you, and you will never be controlled or manipulated by some crotch rocket (which is a big plus).

Number Six: Get and Keep Your Own Place. Don't move into a guy's house. This equals loss of authority. This is a stupid move. Why does this act equal dumb squared? Well, you give a dude all the perks of being married without any commitment. And that's what the date from hell loves: zero commitment. By having as an absolute standard that you will not move in with a guy until you're wed, you will weed out all wankers. The truly great guy will respect you more for your self-control, which, by the way, is a must for any healthy marriage.

Chapter 45.

The Feminists Will Not Like You Reading this Book

Carrie Lukas' new book, *The Politically Incorrect Guide to Women, Sex and Feminism*, just dropped, and I predict that it will get all the feministas' big panties in a major wad. Carrie has done her homework in this easy to read, all bases covered, truly pro-women, hot and pithy tome; and you need to fear, lunatic liberal ladies, because she has facts that are going to challenge your fiction.

I'm sure right now all the anonymous Amazon.com book review attack weirdoes who do not have a life and won't actually read the book but feel compelled to write their inane and uninformed critiques are queuing up to lay into Carrie. They're sweating. And they need to sweat because in this soon-to-be New York Times bestseller, Mrs. Lukas shreds the lies which the female chauvinist pigs (FCP) have sold our nation's fair ladies—I'm talkin' wood chipper style. She shows the women who would be women the true identity of postmodern day feminists: misogynists with vaginas... womyn who not only hate men, but women also.

BTW... have you ever seen a feminist around a womanly woman and not one of her butch buddies who's sporting a Tim Allen haircut? (Question: If feminists and lesbians hate men like they do, why do they try to look like us?) They always have that tsk-tsk, you poor oppressed dupe look on their face . . . y'know, that furrowed brow stare that's a combination of pity and derision. Anyway, back to Lukas' book.

Another cool thing about *The Politically Incorrect Guide to Women, Sex and Feminism* is that it was a young, accomplished woman—who also happens to be a happy wife and mother—who penned this work of non-fiction. These are not the crayon scribblings of some repressed, backwoods, barefoot, unenlightened Ellie Mae Clampett, but rather a girl who got her bachelor's at Princeton, her Masters at Harvard and did it without drinking the lesbians'—I mean the feminists'—Kool Aid.

This book is going to liberate ladies to be ladies; and contrary to the propaganda belched forth via our universities and MSM, there are a whole lot of lassies who:

1. Like being a woman, in a traditional sense. *I'll take a Katharine McPhee over a Hillary any day.
2. Don't think men are the enemy.
3. Like a guy to be a guy, i.e., masculine and not metrosexual. Men who don't have a feminine side. A guy who hasn't "learned to cry."
   *I tried crying in front of my wife one time. It moved her for about twenty seconds. Then she told me to cut the crap and get my act together because she was not going to be married to a poodle. Yes, there are millions of girls who celebrate the difference!
4. (Believe it or not) Like men to the bread winners, who are intellectually robust and who can kick some punk's butt if it needs kickin'. *The other day, a buddy of mine and I nearly opened up a big can a whup a_ _ on a couple of guys who were making obscene gestures toward my wife and daughters. All my girls loved it, and my wife thanked me later.

5. Look to their husband's to provide rather than looking to the feminists' sugar daddy, Uncle Sam.
6. Would like to see a return to chivalry and romance. Who like being courted, pursued, cherished and honored. Who like the guy to pick up the tab (every tab), open the door for them and are not suspicious of flowers and thoughtful gifts.
7. Don't want their vagina turned into a sexual turnstile. Who don't want to be the village bicycle. Who see the benefits of serious sex verses casual sex. Who're not buying the Paris Hilton/Courtney Love/Madonna whore thing. Who can be sexy without being a skank. Who like to retain their respect and power and require a man to show some commitment before he gets to run the bases.
8. Want to get married to a man versus a career. Who still believe that being married to the right guy is good for the soul, the body, the pocket book and their sex life no matter what pop culture and the FCPs have tried to shame them into believing.
9. Want to have a baby before half of their life is history. Who don't want to be in diapers when their child is. *BTW girls, the longer you wait the more difficult it's going to be to get pregnant. If you're waiting strategically 'til your mid 30s–40s well, uh . . . good luck.
10. When they have the baby, they actually want to raise it themselves instead of tossing it into day care or giving it to some nanny who shakes it like a maraca while you're at work. *Speaking of babies, being pro-life is not being anti-woman.
11. Don't feel like they must vote for a woman just because she's a woman.
12. Don't believe being a woman makes them a victim.

I could go on and on singing the praises of this tour de force. This book is destined to do damage to 21st century feminism . . . major, irreparable damage to the likes of NOW, FCP professors and their parrots whose rhetoric and recipes have wrecked the lives of so many, many women around the world.

Do yourself a favor, women who would be women: Buy it, read it, get freed by it and then let your voice be heard, girlfriend.

Chapter 46.

José, can you see?

I love Latin people of every stripe, i.e., European and American. I dig their food, their wine and their women. As a matter of fact, I married a European woman. An Italian to be specific. She's got dark hair, dark eyes, olive skin, more attitude than Sophia Loren and curves you could break your neck on. I'm shvitzing just thinking about her.

The feisty and fun Latino vibe is one of the reasons why I, a pigmentally-challenged man, moved mi familia to Miami. Now that I've been in South Florida for a decade, heck, half of my best friends are Latinos (the other half are imaginary animals that scream curse words in a high pitched mandarin accent at me during the night).

I said all of the above, not to bore you to death with my dorky preferences, life and dementia, but rather to slay any notion that I'm some David Duke xenophobe when it comes to Latinos and their plight before I start to hammer them. Listen, I do not hate Mexicans nor do I hate anyone based upon the color (or lack thereof) of their skin. That's stupid. I follow Dennis Miller's mantra and try to get to know all people better so that I can hate them for deeper and more meaningful reasons.

Speaking of hate . . . it seems like anyone, any longer, who has any standards and won't roll over and wet themselves when their sensibilities and convictions are violated is now deemed a hater. That is, unless of course, the person with the standards is a liberal—and then the person's not a hater but a defender of truth.

Today, everyone who does not blow off and seem completely breezy with our borders being more open than Puffy's pores before he began to use ProActiv is seen as a hater . . . a vile, racist who hates struggling, poor people.

I, for one, think that's pure, uncut nonsense. Everyone nowadays knows that we'd better not be hatin'—but is it really hatin' when all we, the haters, ask the illegal aliens to do are the following:

1. To approach the USA respectfully; this means a) legally and b) in English. I personally am getting pretty tired of hearing, "for English, press one."
2. To not expect us to mangle the Star Spangled Banner just to accommodate you. You, señor, are here, in the US, and now you must speaky English. FYI to the illegal alien: America is a melting pot, so . . . melt. Nuevo himno, my white hiney. It is the National Anthem.
3. To salute—I mean—to *revere*, our country's flag. It's great to have the Mexican flag hanging from your rearview mirror to remind you of your roots, but don't expect that flag to be flown next to the red, white and blue as an equal on our soil, comprende? Why? Well, some Americans still love our nation and the flag for which it stands. You understand . . . it's the reason you're escaping here in the first place, remember?
4. To love our country and dream our American dreams. Not the communist/socialist dream, but the American dream. If you don't, then sneak back across the border. If your former country was and is so bueno and ours is so bogus, then why the heck are you here? Beat it. Rapido.

5. To not come close to tabling the Reconquista crap around us.
6. To understand that to myriads of Americans, you're not an undocumented worker, but an illegal alien. Operative word being, illegal. Il-legal. That means NOT legal. And for those of you who think this is a derogatory term, give me a break. It's not a cut down, or a personal attack, or a means to exclude you from your basic human rights; it's a legal term used to define status of citizenship.
7. To promise that if one of your kids turns into a gangbanger and starts to break our laws that you will whup his butt with that same stick you guys use to split a piñata open and be the first to insist on our justice system giving him what his crimes deserve before he rapes, robs, kills or does anymore damage to one of our legal citizens.
8. And if you're not going to immigrate legally, then you must vow not to protest, tie up our cops and their precious time, clog our highways or demand squat from our cities, states or nation. The only thing you're entitled to is to be arrested and deported. Bear this in mind, por favor.

That's all we haters ask. If you, the illegal alien(s), do the above, you'll find us quite the chipper and accommodating crowd that would love to crack open a Corona with you and wolf down tamales while enjoying a mariachi in the background. However, if you don't play by our nation's distinct terms while you're on our God blessed turf, then don't think it odd if . . .
1. We commence to building a wall on the US/Mexico border that can be seen from outer space, one that'll make the Great Wall of China look like a white picket fence around Dennis the Menace's house.

2. We send bricks to congress, via www.sendabrick.com. For those wishing to send congress a brick to help them get more serious about border security, why not go by Taco Bell while you're at it? Get 'em a taco to send with the bricks. You know, because people get hungry while they're building a wall.
3. We really jump behind the www.MinuteMenHQ.com as they watch our borders more closely than Britney monitors Kevin while he's in Vegas. This will, as it is proven, make it immensely more difficult for you, the illegal alien, to swim, jump or run over here. Speaking of swimming, running and jumping . . . if you guys don't stop flooding across the border to the US, then Mexico will not have a decent Olympic team. Think about it.

And lastly, once again, if anyone, anywhere thinks that the good people's concerns for the law of our land and the defense of our nation can be construed as hatred for aliens or a minority race, I think I can speak for all white people out there and say that if a blue-eyed, blond-haired people began sneaking into our country in droves, violating our laws and jeopardizing our national security, that we would want to kick their skinny white backsides back to whatever Teutonicville they came from.

Chapter 47.

Death Becomes Them

Liberals love being painted as the defender of the underdog. Yeah, if you feel like you are being abused, oppressed, preyed upon, neglected, entitled to something or endangered in any way . . . do not fear! The Dems are here! Their protection extends not only to the human small fry, but also to the translucent hair lice, the gargling nut warbler, a warming globe, a rare venereal crab, a whooping crane's egg, Rudolph's roughage and the need for a rain forest in Iowa.

In addition, many of those in the loopy left will raise unholy hell if hunters hunt animals. Hey, lunatic fringe liberal who prattles on about pity and provision for the poor: In 2005 alone, two of my heartless, conservative hunting buddies and I supplied over seven tons of meat (SEVEN . . . 7 . . . that's 14,000 plus pounds) of low fat/high protein, free range, fresh flesh to the poor—both in Africa and the US. How does that stack up against your personal compassionate outreach last year? Or the last decade? Or the last century? Huh? But that's another topic that I'll save for another column . . . rest assured.

Yeah, the liberals will ramp up to Mach 2, set their hair on fire and will fight, yell, picket, protest and blog their fingers 'til they're bloody for animal rights and for your rights—that is, unless of course, you're an unborn child.

It is with the unborn baby that the "protectors of the weak" morph into the party that wreaks havoc upon the truly helpless. It's interesting to see misty-eyed liberals go quasi-Talibanic for the little animal while they have absolutely no qualms whatsoever endorsing the snuffing out of the life of an unborn tiny human. One of the reasons the barbaric left uses to convince themselves that they're right on the issue of killing that inconvenient "little bugger" (as one of their own calls it) is that it is not yet a person. It's "a wee little squirming blob" that's expendable, which you can root out if you'd like.

One of the things that is really wrecking the "protectors of the weak" BS campaign of killing unborn kids is 3D and 4D ultrasound imagery (Oops. Didn't see that coming, now did you?). These pics and videos are screwing up things for the pro-choicers. Back in the day when they were selling us on the "fetal blob stuff," all we had at our disposal to contradict their nonsense was common sense and a very grainy 2D sonogram. With the advent of ultra slick 3D/4D images, a lot of people are being surprised to see that:

At 8 weeks, this "thing that has no rights whatsoever" (to a liberal) begins to get its groove on, moving and wiggling. Garsh, who'd a thunk it?

At 12 weeks, this "candidate for death" starts yawning (must be overhearing Hillary speak) and performing finger movements (probably also at Hillary). At 20 weeks, this "tissue" starts making facial expressions, such as smiling (who knows . . . maybe it actually feels loved?).

At 24 weeks, the little mister or miss is sucking its thumb, making emotional facial expressions and can stick out its tongue when he or she hears Pelosi blather on CSPAN.

With 3D and 4D ultrasound imaging advancing daily (www.littlesproutimaging.com), how a person can say that an unborn baby is not yet a person and can be killed at Mommy Dearest's discretion is barbarically beyond me.

I guess the left and the pink conservatives callous their hearts to the unborn by rejecting a proposition central to Judeo-Christian thought regarding life and death: namely, that life is intrinsically good, and is therefore, sacrosanct.

Yes, these secular barbaric "tools" see human beings as tools; and if they don't somehow fit instrumentally within the secularists' Darwinian, utilitarian utopia, they get tagged as "inconvenient" and are relegated to the "very expendable" list. That's why abortion is no big deal, and neither is taking the life of a so-called defective child, or suicide, or "mercy killing" a helpless senior. But God help you if you should ever run a boat's prop over a manatee's back! They'll get pissed!

In contrast with the secular "elite," the "stupid," "non-elite" and "archaic" Judeo-Christian constituency views human life (beginning at conception and lasting until the person naturally croaks) as intrinsically good and thus, sacred—not just instrumentally good.

The Judeo-Christian community believes that all people—from the embryo to the elderly, including severely developmentally disabled, people in comas and everything in between—have dignity and value. As Robert George said, "Their significance is not based upon what they can do, or how they make us feel or whether or not we approve of their quality of life, but principally because they live."

And not only does the Party of Death (as Ramesh Ponnuru calls the liberals in his latest book, *The Party of Death*) advocate the death of the unborn and the inconvenient, but they also want your tax dollar to pay for their death wishes, for all parents to butt out of their teen age daughter's abortion plans and for the US to continue to stay left of Europe when it comes to abortion on demand. Consider all the above, those of you on the left and the right who cherish the unborn more than a sea cow, when you cast your vote during the midterms and when you're looking for a candidate for '08.

Chapter 48.

An Open Letter to Illegal Immigrants

If I were a Mexican stuck in Mexico, I, too, would grab a jug of aqua, stuff fistfuls of tortillas into a bandana, then tie that knap sack onto the end of a long stick and start my slog north for the Promised Land.

What would be the rationale for my exodus from Santa Ana land? Well, one big reason is the zero opportunity in Mexico. Mexico's economic future is about as bright as Leif Garrett's singing career. I'm talking there is nada for the average José. Look, Vicente Fox can only hire out so many pool boys, chefs, drivers, maids, migrant map makers and mistresses. For the rest of the national workforce . . . well, you're pretty much SOL.

Eclipsing the economic disaster are two other reasons why, if I were a Mexican living in Mexico, I'd be putting the Sierra Madres in my rearview mirror and heading for Marfa: namely, Telemundo and Univision. Yes, if those were the only two channels I could watch on my black and white Philco after a 16-hour day of picking mangos in exchange for two chickens, I would walk through the desert for hundreds of miles, brave banditos, eat horny toads, drink mud, bake in the sun, swim the Rio Grande, scale the Big Bend mountains and wrestle pumas just to get away from that tacky entertainment and to get here to the States where I could enjoy

Fox News and Verses. Therefore, as compassionate conservatives, we've got to cut these guys some slack. We, too, would want out of such a dysfunctional banana republic.

Now, having said that, let me address mi amigos who want to move into our amazing Land-O-Plenty: Would you mind immigrating legally and learning English? Because, you see, our legal citizens are getting increasingly fed up with your criminal relocation dreams. That's right. Our American buddies on the Arizona, California, New Mexico and Texas borders are especially sick of:

• Having their land trashed like a hotel room after Motley Crüe spent the weekend there (one Indian reservation picks up trash to the tune of six tons a day. Would you please stop that? It's rude, and it's threatening the existence of a certain lizard and the Sonoran Pronghorn antelope. Thanks).

- Having their ranches' fencing routinely cut and vandalized.
- Having to pick up your pill bottles, used needles and syringes.
- Having to find the half-eaten remains of their pets left from one of your impromptu BBQs.
- Having their homes burglarized.
- Having their daughters raped.
- Having their vehicles stolen.
- Having their property values plummet.
- Having their sedate streets become unsafe and requiring their children to be placed under lock and key after sunset.
- Having to pick up and discard Muslim prayer rugs and literature strafed about the place. (BTW . . . when did so many Catholic Mexicans convert to Islam? I didn't get that brief. Would you explain that to me?)
- Having the arduous and unpleasant chore of scraping human feces off their front lawns in the morning.

An Open Letter to Illegal Immigrants

Call us Americans fastidious, but we no likey the aforementioned; and the above is not causing us to take a shining to your desires to resettle here.

Let me help would-be Mexican immigrants understand exactly where we're coming from. Our nation's leniency regarding immigration has been used as a night stick to whup our own butt. Our nation's compassionate openness, plus the corrupt incompetence of the former INS, plus our government's greed for foreign capital equaled a rolled-out welcome mat for the 9/11 terrorists and other thieves and thugs who looked to use us while they attempted to destroy us. So excuse us, por favor, if we don't seem too giddy about receiving new guests into our home; we're still cleaning up after the last ones who tried to destroy the place.

Look, if you want to come here and visit, work or possibly live in the US of A, you must understand that it is a privilege. Be very clear on one fact: it is NOT a right. We don't have to do anything.

In addition, we want people who dream the American dream (once again—in English), who crave what we crave and who will approach us respectfully, legally and . . . if you don't mind terribly . . . pardon my redundancy—in English. And get this straight: Our demand for a more stringent border has nothing—*nothing!*—to do with xenophobia. Rather, it is rooted in a love for our country. We like it here. We see it as a privilege and an honor to live here. And we want to make sure that when letting others join us in this privilege and honor, we are rewarding the credible who have waited, not the criminal who has manipulated. So, my advice is to immigrate correctly. Do it right . . . and if you choose not to—**don't** think it unkind if you get tossed on your head right back **to** where you came from.

Chapter 49.

Go Beyond the Pavement

I love ticking off as many vapid, anti-American and anti-traditional values blowhards as I can. It is one of the chief joys of my life. However, sometimes I need a reprieve from the rancor and the hell razing.

Aside from needing a break from the bellicosity that is my life, I need a break from the place where I live, i.e. Miami. This place is more plastic than Joan River's face, breasts, ear lobes, tummy, or . . . yecch! I'm sorry. I just made myself vomit. Excuse me for a sec . . . okay, I'm back.

In addition to the synthetic scene here in South Florida, the metrosexual madness down here is so sassy and solid it leaves a redneck refugee like me shaking like a junkie for a testosterone reality fix away from the weapons-grade foolishness that unfortunately inundates one of the most beautiful spots on the planet.

Also, I get ill thinking about having to go to the mall, again, and having to ford through all the mall rats, with their fake (or real, I don't care) Louis Vuitton purses, Gucci shades, and their angst over whether they should get "A/X's skinny jeans or Abercrombie's new ones." Yeah, having to share air with these helix-missing morons and being forced to overhear how bad their lives reek as they scream on their cell phones leaves me with an intense desire to get the hell outta Dodge. Y'know what I'm sayin'?

Furthermore (and I know I'm not supposed to say this), I get weary at times of talk radio and TV talk shows, which are quickly becoming my life. Doesn't it get old, occasionally, hearing the left and right go at each other night after night after night after night? Call me a wussy, but since I don't drop acid or smoke ganja anymore I need to escape.

A cruise is out of the question for me. Being on a disease-laced, slow moving diarrhea ship filled with stretch pant wearing, buffet loving, overweight, pink-skinned drunks who are paraded like lemmings from one overpriced port to the next is not my idea of recreating.

Nothing, as far as I'm concerned, does more for me than getting away and going hunting with my family and friends. Putting massive distance between me and the mall, my cell phone and my e-mail and going beyond the pavement in pursuit of the planet's magnificent game animals or birds is b-e-a-u-tiful to me.

What do I like about it?

My cell phone usually doesn't work.

Just getting out in the wild connects me back to my primal spiritual and physical roots. God didn't create Adam to live in a condo. He made a feral crib for his first man to live and whup it up in with Eve. There is something that the undomesticated does to me that no Lysol disinfected, five star hotel can provide.

Everything slows down. I'm forced to chill out. I'm not going mach 2 with my hair on fire. I'm forced to shut up and quit screaming. I'm forced to breathe, and the air I inhale in the woods is clean and not some germ-laden, stale, fart loaded, re-circulated office oxygen (I office out of my home).

My senses come alive and are taken to a higher level by pursuing my prey. My eyes, ears, nose, feet and hands kick into gear like they don't when I'm sitting like a drooling, giggling, Corona drinking zombie watching Seinfeld on my couch.

It makes me get disciplined. To be a successful hunter requires strictness. To shoot a rifle, shotgun, pistol or bow well takes commitment. To successfully stalk a big game animal and make a clean and lethal shot takes additional dedication. To hunt dangerous game animals requires that I be a seriously focused little monkey. To sit quietly for hours takes Tibetan monk like tenacity. To chase wild boar through a swamp, cougars over miles of desert mountains, and elk where the air is thin means I've gotta work out during the week, or I'm going to be more lost than K-Fed watching Bret Hume. The above de rigueur explains why I don't see too many crack heads on the hunting fields. My sport demands you have your act together.

Hunting changes lives. I've seen it several times. I have seen bored adults and kids come alive when the hunt commences. I've watched idiots on drugs lay them down for good because they got a greater buzz hunting with good people than they did snorting crank with their butt munch friends in Hialeah. BTW, for the too cool teen or twenty-something who might not think hunting can be as thrilling as drugs, come with me and confront a 350lb POed wild boar, or come to the glades and hunt gators out of an air boat, or take a shot at a grizzly with a bow, or face up to a hippo out of the water with a double rifle. I guarantee ecstasy, 'shrooms, and a crystal has never, can never and will never give you the buzz that these situations will. You'll mess your pants. Give it a try, girlfriend. You'll be sweating like Ahmadinejad in church.

I connect with friends and family on a deeper level. Life's busy in the city. Sometimes, even the "good" relationships we have with friends and family are about as shallow as a creek in Death Valley. The campfire allows for communication that you do not get when the idiot box is on and everyone is running in fifty different directions. If it weren't for my dad taking me hunting every year when I was a kid, I probably wouldn't really even know him (which might be a plus for him, but would be a huge minus for me). I feed hundreds of poor people with high protein, low fat, yummy flesh that comes from my kills. I guarantee that I and just three of my hunting compadres feed way more hungry people via hunting than your typical group of 1,000 bleeding heart, yarbling, anti-hunters ever have or will.

There are very few loony liberals. Another great blessing regarding hunting is that I seldom, if ever, run into secular, "progressive," pluralistic, relativistic, big government loving, anti-military, God and country hating leftists.

Yes, when I'm looking for a break I bound into the swamp, brush or woods with gun or bow in tow in pursuit of one of our planet's amazing game animals. Nothing, absolutely nothing, restores my soul like everything that surrounds the sport of hunting with friends and family. As a matter of fact, my 79-year old dad, three of my closest buddies and I are gearing up for a great Maine black bear hunt next week.

Hunters, get away this fall and winter. Don't let this season not see you and yours in the woods. Also, join the NRA, Safari Club International and Ted Nugent's United Sportsman of America. Kick your cash into these organizations that keep PETA and other paltry, paranormal, anti-hunting organizations at bay and help us keep alive our great American heritage of hunting.

Chapter 50.

The Re-Texification of Doug Giles
By Doug Giles

Living in Miami for the last ten years has been interesting. Being a transplant from Texas to South Florida, I've come to learn a lot from the multitudinous left-leaning lemmings in Miami. Things like the US sucks, Europe is yippee, traditional values are for the vapid and non-evolved, there is no right or wrong (just pleasure and pain) and that terrorists are angry because of... uh... something we must've done. Yeah, it seems nowadays, here on the Gold Coast where I live, as if I am constantly having to defend classic America, God, our founding principles and the war on terror on a 24/7 basis.

Having had it "up to here" with the secularized rancor I regularly experience, I had to have a little retreat. Where did I go to get away from the "progressive" paranormals who populate Florida's floating sod? I went back to the motherland, Texas.

Yeah, when I needed to clear my head and get a dose of hope for my country, I headed northwest to the Lone Star State. Being the hunter that I am, I called my dad and we went deer hunting at my friend Phil Mason's ranch in the heart of the Texas hill country. Not only did we get to successfully hunt whitetail, axis deer, bobcat and black buck antelope on

Phil's beautiful place, but I also got to see and hear pro-US sentiments coming from my hunting compadres.

It was weird (in a good sense) to observe and listen to people who are still:

1. Proud of the US. The Texans I was fortunate to hang with are not blind to the few (compared to other whacked nations) faults we have in our land. Having said that, they still think we are an awesome country and not the Great Satan that the lunatic left and Islam deem us to be. Yes, the guys I hunted with have not surrendered to "the US sucks" cheer that the secular regressives keep trying to shove up everyone's tail pipe.

2. Hard working. During my jaunt in Tejas, I didn't see too many people loitering and trying to suck off the entitlement tit. As a matter of fact, I found a low tolerance for low output people. They believe that if you work your butt off, no matter what your stripe, life pays you back in spades.

    Not only do they believe such a supposed "arcane notion," but they are also examples of success that flowered from an initial rough start. I heard no entitlement mentality while visiting. And another thing ... when we went into town for supplies, the store employees weren't talking on their stupid cell phones to their lovers while they smacked gum and looked at you weird when you asked them for a little help. The employees were nice (imagine that), well-dressed and ready to help the customer. Unbelievable! What a time warp I stepped into.

3. Church going. Another thing that fish slapped me was the fact that all the guys I hunted with are church-goers. They aren't tree humping, hippy pantheists. They are not pluralistic, irrational, global group huggers with insane, geo-ecclesiastical expectations.

They aren't the "make it up as you go" spiritual goons who gobble up oxygen on South Beach. They are God-fearing, Bible-believing, imperfect people who believe (and worship publicly) a perfect God and Christ. What a breath of fresh air compared to the putrid and puerile O2 I have to breathe that's belched forth from the atheists and the anything-but-Christ cabal that constitutes secular South Florida.

4. Gun owning and toting. This too, for me, was a major perk to behold. I had indeed found my tribe. Yeah, I had landed within a group of people who love guns, who buy guns (many of them of various calibers, gauges, types and actions), who use guns, who tote guns and who make zero apologies for the aforementioned. They understand the Second Amendment and relish what it affords them as citizens and sportsmen. Ka-Pow.

5. Very pleasant. A crazy thing that I noticed that was different to my South Florida surroundings was how friendly everyone was. How weird. I didn't hear people yelling and screaming because the barista at Starbucks put $1/8^{th}$ of an inch too much foam on their skinny cappuccino. I did not see the middle finger flying with more regularity than a ferret turns its head. Where I live in Miami, I have an acquaintance who has used his middle finger so much it is actually shorter and thinner than all his other fingers (there should be a tax write off for that somewhere).

While in Texas, I heard things like "please," and "thank you," and "yes, sir" and "yes, ma'am" . . . not just coming from octogenarians of yesteryear either but from (believe it or not) peers and teens. *Teens* of all people! Yeah, the young people there were not some sneering, chip on their shoulder, 5o cent

wannabes ready with an F-bomb if you happened to look at them for a nanosecond.
6. Military honoring and terrorist hating. The Texan brethren I had the good fortune to hunt with also had in tow an utter disdain for all Islamic miscreants who wish us ill. And you know what else was cool? They were up-front and didn't try to sterilize their contempt and their wishes for death to all those who would try to derail the American dream for them, their children and their children's children.

One last thing that struck me while hunting in Texas was the many young soldiers I saw at the airport. These young warriors at DFW walked with heads held high and were greeted and thanked by the many Texans who saw them cruising through the airport. B-e-a-u-tiful.

Compared to South Florida, Texas was weird—but in a good way. To be honest, I have been severely tempted to move back. However, I kind of think I might lose my edge if I left the whacky waste places of zany South Florida. Who knows? What I do know is that I'm proud to be from Texas, proud to know such people and proud to be a redneck rather than a pink, yellow or no neck, rootless and feckless, secularist regressive.

Chapter 51.

Raising Boys That Feminists Will Hate

Parent, if you have a young son and you want him to grow up to be a man, then you need to keep him away from pop culture, public school and a lot of Nancy Boy churches. If metrosexual pop culture, feminized public schools and the effeminate branches of evanjellycalism lay their sissy hands on him, you can kiss his masculinity good-bye—because they will morph him into a dandy.

Yeah, mom and dad, if . . . if . . . you dare to raise your boy as a classic boy in this castrated epoch, then you've got a task that's more difficult than getting a drunk Ted Kennedy to hit the urinal at Chili's.

Get it right, mom and dad—you are rowing against the flotsam and jetsam of Sally River. I hope you have a sturdy ideological paddle and some serious forearms because postmodernism is determined to keep your boy and his testosterone at bay. Yes, they will attempt at every turn to either drill it or drug it out of him.

Parent, if you're groping for a creedal oar to help you stem the increasingly stem-less effete environment, I've got a novel idea: Howzabout going back to the Bible, in particular the book of Genesis, and see what God the Father created His initial kid to be. Check this out:

Then God said, "Let the earth bring forth the living creature according to its kind: cattle and creeping thing and beast of the earth, each according to its kind"; and it was so. And God made the beast of the earth according to its kind, cattle according to its kind, and everything that creeps on the earth according to its kind. And God saw that it was good. Then God said, "Let Us make man in Our image, according to Our likeness; let them have dominion over the fish of the sea, over the birds of the air, and over the cattle, over all the earth and over every creeping thing that creeps on the earth." So God created man in His own image; in the image of God He created him; male and female He created them. Then God blessed them, and said to them, "Be fruitful and multiply; fill the earth and subdue it; have dominion over the fish of the sea, over the birds of the air, and over every living thing that moves on the earth. (Gen.1.24-28.)

Born to be Wild.

First off, parents, please note that the cradle God created for His firstborn was rough country—a thorny, critter-laden and butt-kicking badland. God wanted His boy brought up in undomesticated surroundings. The feral fashioned something in God's first boy, Adam, that Xbox, the mall and cell phones just couldn't provide to the charge under His tutelage.

Yeah, God's earthy 2IC was directly connected to the Spirit of the Wild. Adam lived in primitive partnership with untamed beasts, birds, big lizards and monster sharks. This is the way it was. And God said, "It is good!" Imagine that: good being equated to having no anti-bacterial gel, no bike helmets, no Trans Fatty acids, no poodles, no motorized scooters, no concrete and no Will and Grace. I know this doesn't sound like "paradise" for postmodern pantywaists who are immoral, lazy, stupid and fat, but it was God's—and His primitive son's—idea of "Yippee Land."

So what do we learn from this preliminary little Bible nugget, children? The lesson is clear: If you want your boy to step away from the pusillanimous pomo pack, then you might want to get Junior outdoors, beyond the pavement, and let the created order carve its mark into your son.

I don't have boys, but I make certain that my two alpha teen-aged females, along with my wife and I, get a regular dose of the irregular wild. Our lives consist of large quantities of surfing in shark infested waters, biking in the backwoods, workouts on the beach, hunting in the sweltering swamps of the everglades for wild boar, fishing the brimming waters of South Florida and treks into the African bush. Why do we make the financial commitment and time-laden efforts to get away from the Miami metropolis? Well, call us weak, but we need it for our souls, our sanity and our spirits in this increasingly plastic place. The spiritual and ethical moorings that nature affords us cannot be found in the tame and lame wastelands of civilization.

So, take the time—no—make the time, parents of the peculiar Y chromosomes—to venture out with your boy . . . away from the city, away from the tidy and predictable . . . and watch what happens to your son as he separates from the prissy and is forced to interface with the primal. It is magical.

Born to Rule.

God's initial earth boy was born to dominate creation and to exercise authority over the planet. God designed His first terrestrial son to be a leader, to take charge, to exert influence. Yaweh didn't construct Adam to be a passive clod, some indolent handout addict who abnegated his responsibility to other people or institutes; but rather, Adam was to be a bold and imaginative chief. This is the very thing the misandrists hate in men and are trying desperately to curb in your kid, namely, this can-do spirit.

Parent, you should encourage your bambino to lead, compete and conquer. Whether it is subduing his backyard, his dirty bedroom or an opposing team, or mastering a musical instrument, a textbook or a chore—your son should learn to govern, be the champion and strive for excellence in accomplishment in all that he does.

Look, according to Scripture, your son is a natural born leader who will naturally want to control. It is only, and I mean only, when boys are cowed by abusive authority, Ritalined out of their brains or indoctrinated to believe this God-given behavior is bad that they turn into the followers, the veritable sheeples of stupid cultural morays, folding to high pressure peers and ideological BS. With the leader funk removed from their trunk, now the boys become tofu for the man haters. Now they become malleable little spongy playthings and are no longer steel-willed competitive leaders. Yes, they become nice, placid cooperators and doormats to fools and foes. God never intended a boy, your boy, to be this.

Therefore, parent, your job is twofold: 1) Unleash the leadership beast within your boy and 2) Superintend it to make sure it doesn't get weird; rather ensure it is used for the purpose of justice, truth, provision and protection. Take God's lead and show your son how to exercise dominion rather than how to get in touch with his feminine side. Maw and Paw, stand against the swill of society that seeks to erase this grand masculine trait from your little treasure and teach that kid how to be a constructive conqueror.

Born to Cultivate.

The Garden of Eden that God allotted Adam was not some dorm room that he was licensed to trash, but a place he was "to tend and keep" (Gen.2.16). Adam was to cultivate that which he had subdued. With his leadership came the responsibility and accountability to God to take that which was under his care and make it better. Can you say better? I knew you could.

This means, mom and dad, it's cool for you to have expectations of your kid about his role in your family and in this game of life: it is to enhance that which is good and to not whiz on everything people have worked for. Let little Johnny know that whatever gets tossed to him is to be brought into greater order, usefulness and beauty. Make sure he gets the message that he's to do it. You heard me . . . him. Johnny. Not the government, not mommy, not his nanny, not his church, or his lawyer—Johnny is to get his act together. Johnny is to make the place shine. And Johnny is to feel really bad if he does not make things better and people prosper.

Therefore, parent of he that liveth in the God-blessed testosterone fog, train your son that he is not free to use, abuse, abandon, desert, ignore, overlook, disregard, forget, avoid, mistreat or neglect that which gets placed under his care—and if . . . if . . . he does, he is to have his backside whupped. What am I saying? Your boy needs to slowly begin to feel the weight of masculine responsibility on his shoulders and learn how to get his skinny legs strong enough so that he doesn't drop it. BTW parents . . . it won't crush him. He's tougher than you're being led to believe.

Discipline your boy to fend for himself and others as if there were no government, no church, no school, no courts, no therapy, no drugs and no cops to lean on to make things all better. Yeah, raise him to feel as if it is his duty to be the provider, to educate his children, to defend his family and nation, to judge disputes, to offer worship, to give spiritual advice and comfort—and to do all of this without acting like a chick.

The wild thing that'll happen is you'll see little Johnny turn into big John who brings to the table more than waxed eyebrows and manicured hands and who's always looking to the ladies to lead him. Instead, you'll have raised a son who brings to the table emotional strength, physical toughness, firm correction, world wisdom, constructive criticism and ethical principles—and one who does it while having a heck-of-a-lot-of fun. This cultivating spirit will, by fiat, make him a leader wherever he happens to go, and you know, you know, the long-toothed feminists will really, really, really hate that.

Born to Slay Dragons.

In Genesis chapter three, when our first parents got tossed out of the sweet haven of Eden's crib, God said He was going to redeem this hamartialogical mess by raising up a Son who is to crush the serpent. Where God's first man, Adam, blew it by not being the dragon slayer, His second man, the Last Adam, took care of business and turned the malevolent slithering one into a grease stain.

If you as a parent take your cue from Christ in raising your son, then your boy will grow up to be a mini-me slayer of serpents. He will not be a pacifist in the face of evil. He will not roll over and wet himself when confronted by crap. He will not play the wimp when faced with difficult situations.

Look, I know it's hard for some of us to square Christ with slaying dragons ... given all the androgynous, soft-focused paintings of Jesus that we've had jammed into our psyches for the last few centuries. However, if, if, you take Scripture straight (as I do my whiskey), the man of peace is painted as an eschatological warrior who has great joy in giving the devil hell. No matter how hard the softies try to make Christ out to be the benign, bearded lady raconteur, or a 19th century liberal, or a 21st century feminist, the exegetical fact remains: If you take the holy text in its entirety, He does not fit into the effete mold.

Therefore, mom and dad, have your boy get used to confronting nonsense—first and foremost in himself. Gear him up to be a fighter and defender of that which is just and good. Let him play, as one author said, with toy weapons instead of Barbies (if you can find any). He's not going to turn into a terrorist. It's not going to warp his wheel. Your son has to learn that he is growing up in difficult times that demand he be able to deal with "snakes." Yes, your boy needs to learn not only to be nice, but also to be strong, sacrificial and courageous. You know . . . the very God-given and nature-expected stuff that the female chauvinist pigs are seeking to sift from him.

Born to be Wise.

One way to foment the female chauvinist pigs is to make sure, mom and dad, that your son is incredibly smart. You must make certain that he not only has a well-fed wild streak, a willingness and ability to lead in life, that whatever he gets his hands on prospers, and that he will tackle evil wherever and whenever it raises its ugly head, but that he is also the most well read-boy on the block.

Parent, if your son stays dumb (and I'm not referring to children with learning disabilities) then he boosts the malicious stereotype that the fems are shoving up our society's tailpipe, and he unwittingly sets the stage for a worse mañana, at least as far as masculinity goes. Mom and dad (and especially dad), don't give the female chauvinist pigs any ground by pitting one form of masculinity (leading) against another form (reading).

Parents, teach your rough and ready boy that:

1. Serious studying is not just for Poindexters and geeks.

2. Studying, learning and holding intellectual discussions are all part of being masculine.
3. The intellectual target you're aiming for him to strike doesn't look like Tommy Boy or Homer Simpson; but rather more like King David, William Wallace and Sir Winston Churchill.
4. It takes guts and nuts to tackle the various sciences, and no matter what his Beavis and Butthead friends think, serious study is not for "wusses." As a matter of fact, it is just the opposite. Reading, meditating, gaining understanding and knowledge and staying abreast of what has happened—and what is happening—on this world's stage is so hard that the effeminate, the little Sallys, the prancing, petite male poodles won't do it; they actually avoid it like Rosie O'Donnell does Jenny Craig.
5. God intends for him to be sharp and to not be a bastardization of his great gender. Then, Daddy-O, go to work to get your kid a killer library. Spend the cash!
6. The rowdy realm of ideas and debates can be just as fun as any sport. In fact, one of my greatest joys is when I get to go toe-to-toe on the radio, TV or over dinner with a flaming liberal or raging atheist. Yeah, it is right up there with hunting Africa's green hills . . . nearly.

Finally, parent, can you imagine the angst when Hollywood and the multitudinous, hijacked-by-feminists universities can no longer play the stooge card when it comes to men because the sons you have raised have engaged their brains and have not opted for anti-intellectualism? Can you picture, mom and dad, how the faces of the female chauvinist pigs will contort and how their stomachs will gurgle with acid as the stereotype they've worked so long and hard to prop up no longer works because you, the parent, have raised your son to be intellectually astute?

I have a dream!

Born to Reflect the Majesty of God.

Parents, one great way to have Johnny not turn into J. Alexander (or Jay Manuel for that matter) is to take serious stock of the male role models he's around. Your son is going to imitate someone, so make certain it isn't Eminem, 50 Cent, Barry Bonds, Johann van der Sloot, Richard Simmons or John Couey. This is not rocket science. But it is a science. It's simple: if you don't want your son to be emasculated or macho-stupid, be careful who you allow him to walk with on his schlep. Monkey see, monkey do.

BTW, can some of you girls stop imitating guys? Please? Like . . . now? The other day I saw this Hispanic chick cruising on a Harley. Her gut was hanging over her way-too-low-cut jeans, she had a cigarette dangling from the corner her mouth, and she was sporting more tattoos than a Maasai warrior. I had to do a double take because I thought it was my gardener with a wig and some Frederick's inserts. Yikes!

Also, girls, if you want to celebrate your "freedom" from misogynist's constructs by smoking a cigar, don't smoke a .62 ring gauge maduro 8" Churchill. Stay somewhere south of .36. I know you're not supposed to trust men; but trust me—you'll look better.

Now, back to role models for your son. Even I have role models in case I drift to the effete dark side. There are eight in particular who help me keep my testosterone in focus and my boys intact.

1. Larry the Cable Guy. He keeps me tethered to my beloved redneck roots that are under constant attack down here in the oh so sassy South Florida. Git-R-Done, Larry.

2. Dennis Miller. Miller keeps the wise guy alive and well in me, which is a must if you want to mess with the FCPs and have the attitude necessary to navigate the Sargasso morass the feminuts spew forth.
3. Ted Nugent. Ditto. The Nuge also brings to the table an enviable love for hunting, guns and all that is wild and free. His music, books, concerts and our conversations keep my primitive man in fine shape.
4. Os Guinness. He takes the dumb out of Christendom.
5. R.C. Sproul. He is an apt destroyer of atheistic nonsense and a brilliant communicator of the essentials of Christianity.
6. My dad. He loved one woman, raised four kids and put them through college, and at age 79 is sharp, strong and one helluva big game fisherman. Tight lines and screaming reels, Dad.
7. Several dead guys for several reasons. To name a few: Winston Churchill, Nicolai Fechin and Teddy Roosevelt. And last but certainly not least . . .
8. God. I know following His flawless lead is most of the time an exercise in futility, but the Unseen One is a great example of masculine uniqueness. He's wild and He's wise . . . a warrior, a king, a prankster, a healer and a father. We are made in His image and should reflect his glory.

Now, my personal role models might not be the ones you'd choose; but the point for you as a parent is to be one for your son—and get some others who will help you forge your son into the force he's been called to become. Mom & Dad, by simply taking control (taking control, taking control) of who your boy hangs out with, what you let him watch, read and listen to, you can help him find his masculine groove and pursue it with vigor while blowing off the effeminate funk of the FCPs.

Chapter 52.

Can the British Still Call a Cigarette a Fag?

When it comes to unleashing humorous and scathing vocal invectives, Jesus was King of Kings. Yes, the Prince of Peace punk'd people like no other could. Would He have used the word "faggot" in one of His verbal chainsaw massacres upon the political and ecclesiastical morons of His day? Absolutely . . . not.

No, Christ would not have called some soulless, Aqua Net addicted, duplicitous politician who hires anti-Christ, homely bloggers a fag. That would needlessly offend the homosexual community by comparing them to a skanky politician. Having said that, I have no doubt Christ would have cranked out a cut down on a first century Edwardsian equivalent that would have sawn the boy down to the ground—Dorothy Hamill haircut and all.

Many don't see this side of Christ because they're biblically illiterate. Being dee-tee-dee, they get their cue regarding "what Jesus would do" via the brand spankin' new, pretty and PCified, 21st century Christ they have created just for their squishy flesh.

We all know this new Jesus. He's the positive motivational speaker/Savior who says, "howdy doo," has Mitt Romney-like eternal hair, loves kittens and grins so much his gums are drier than Gandhi's sandals. In addition, our new Hey-Suess would never say anything to offend anyone; or if he did, it would be about "they and them" but not "you and you."

If you take Scripture straight (as I do my Johnny Blue) and you get no help from some PC slathered priest and simply read the Gospels (imagine that!), you will see that our loving, compassionate life-giving Savior also skewered His opponents, His friends and a of lot supposed "earnest" seekers like Wolfgang Puck would a small pig.

If you're a conservative who purports to be a Christian, then you're to get your behavioral and communication cues from Christ—not some politician (past or present). And FYI . . . the Lamb of God was no Lamb Chop in word or deed.

Not only did Jesus perform some outrageous and scandalous acts of compassion, but also as stated, He was a verbally vicious warrior when necessary. He wasn't some squeegee cleaned, wind testing cliché weaver of fuzzy phrases. He said stuff that made people want to kill Him, and y'know . . . if I remember the story correctly, I think they eventually did.

Sweet baby Jesus grew up into a rowdy man who personally attacked people, both in their presence and absence, and being the fun-loving Savior that He is, He did His dissecting primarily via exaggeration and caricature. As a matter of fact, His shtick (if the Trinity doesn't mind me calling it "a shtick," which they don't because I'm one of Their favorites), was one of outrageous exaggerations.

As Douglas Wilson points out in his brilliant book, *A Serrated Edge*, in regard to communication, Jesus . . .

1. Roamed from mild Horatian irony to His preferred Agent Orange approach.
2. Portrayed incongruities in a blistering humorous light, and it wasn't because He was a funny man. He

was using humor (remember humor?) as a polemical weapon.
3. Applied offensive humor for necessary controversy. His illustrations and attacks were for the express purpose of getting the party started. Things were oh so boring back then, and someone had to shatter a beer mug or two.
4. Didn't weep all the time when He saw sin and hypocrisy. As a matter of fact, He didn't weep near as much as many sniveling non-prophets today do. Christ's usual MO was a) whip the culprits or b) ridicule the crap out of them. Make them cartoon boys. Jesus, as Wilson points out, understood that kindness to wolves is hostility to sheep.
5. Made fun of how insincere people prayed and fasted. You wouldn't fall asleep at His CPAC speech.
6. He used ethnic humor to prove His point. Try that today.
7. Called one nice lady a dog. A dog! A self cleaning, butt sniffing, vomit eating, flea riddled dog (Snap!).
8. Didn't engage in smarmy, pipe smoking, "your turn/my turn" arguments most of the time. He simply let fly and then left the room, not seeking any extended dialogue with dilatory dimwits.
9. Shotgun blasted those insufferable critics who were never satisfied.
10. Ripped into the Pharisees in the book of Matthew chapter 23, his magnum opus that makes Ann Coulter look like a kitty.

All of the above is from the one who so love the world that He laid down His life for us.

And don't even get me started on the words the prophets and apostles used to whittle down the wusses of their day. They popped off with analogies, especially the prophets, not unlike those with which a stevedore would serve up. Most pastors and politicos wouldn't even touch these passages in public. But men inspired of God did, and they rocked the house. I wonder if you and I could roll with these boys. Selah.

Let me ask the Ann pooh-poohers on the Right a question: What exactly is one allowed to say or not say? Can I say pooh-pooh? What words are verboten? What about phrases? Analogies? What about body parts? Hair? Pot bellies? Tones? Can we have a tone when we talk? Can we roll our eyes? Snicker? Yawn? Can we cough, "bull$#@&" when we hear something ridiculous? Can the British still call a cigarette a fag?

Please, help us endangered brutish beasts of the baser sort to understand the Nancy world of civility that some are sweetly rollerblading into. Also, for clarification, which pundit(s), blogger(s) or radio show host(s) now determine what's cool and what's not cool? Will it be a group thing or do you have one Dandy you're looking to?

I think all the stink that's been made on the Right regarding Coulter's joke is simply envious folks trying to get their slice of the Ann power pie. Of course, they'll never confess that because envy is the one sin people never like or admit they have.

What is Envy? Envy is, as Thomas Aquinas said, "sorrow at another's good." Someone who is centered can watch another person righteously prosper and not hate him or her for it.

Not so with the envious. When the me-monkey sees someone else excel, they are slapped in the face with the reality that they're getting dogged. Instead of sucking it up and working harder and smarter, they allow their pride to fuel their wounded wittle spirit. This sets the dejected one down a path of disparagement of the prosperous that eventually morphs into the desire to destroy the person who is trumping them.

Look, the way I judge my co-belligerents in the conservative cause is this: Can they, in an enlightened and entertaining way, wreak havoc upon the secularists who are attempting to hijack this God blessed nation? I don't care whether or not they're my style or if I agree with all that they do. If I'm in a bar fight and I'm getting my butt handed to me, I'm not looking for perfection; I'm looking for a fellow warrior who can cave in the skull of my enemy. And that's what Ann does. She decimates the Left . . . and for that, I salute her.

So . . . has anybody seen any good movies lately?

Chapter 53.

Tasty Christian Books for The Serious Meat Eater

If the Christian wants to be a practical player in the 21st century then he's going to have to put some spiritual meat on his skinny bones. With a lot of pulpits occupied by puppets who are poisoned with political correctness and have bought a therapeutic approach to ministry, there's about as much "meat" in postmodern churches as there is animal protein at a PETA party. Since the substantial pickins have become quite slim within certain craven and capitulating sectors of Christendom, the believer who wants to live for something worth Christ's death has got to seek sustenance elsewhere. That's where the books come in.

The following book list is not a cure-all, nor is it exhaustive; and although I do not agree with everything within the individual books, if you take the time to read them and meditate upon their contents, they will:

1. Shoot hope into your soul,
2. Establish God's call as THE priority in life,
3. Breathe faith into your flagging spirit,
4. Put balls on believers,
5. Hand you a workable blueprint for action,
6. Shore up sagging convictions,
7. Give you a new attitude,

8. Hand you answers for tough questions,
9. Build you into an adept spiritual warrior and
10. Make you more proficient in prayer.

For '07, why don't you put down your little feel good tofu type of books and get these bad mambajambas for the new year?

Paradise Restored: A Biblical Theology of Dominion, by David Chilton. This is an excellent read regarding the biblical hope that good will triumph over evil in time and not just eternity. That's even with Pelosi in the House and Barack Obamanation on the rise. Chilton slays the inactive, marginalized Christian theology that wants to do nothing more than sit and wait for the rapture, while simultaneously fueling the victorious believer with the biblical premise that Christianity is the answer for the world's woes and will be successful in its mission. If you're tired of the typical end of the world, doom and gloom, pin the tail on the beast TBN prophecy novels, well then, this Bud is for you. From Eden to the cross and beyond, David Chilton unfolds an eschatology of victory. Good luck finding one, though, as it's out of print. But believe me, it's worth the search.

The Call: Finding and Fulfilling The Central Purpose to Your Life, by Os Guinness. *The Call* continues to stand as a classic, reflective work on life's purpose. Rick Warren's book is lame compared to this soul-plumbing work. Bestselling author Os Guinness goes beyond our surface understanding of God's call and addresses the fact that God has a specific calling for our individual lives. Why am I here? What is God's call in my life? How do I fit God's call with my own individuality? How should God's calling affect my career, my plans for the future, and my concepts of success? Guinness now helps the reader discover answers to these questions. According to Guinness, "No idea short of God's call can ground and fulfill the truest human desire for purpose and fulfillment." With tens of thousands of readers to date, *The Call* is for all who desire a purposeful, intentional life of faith. (From the back cover)

The Church Impotent: The Feminization of Christianity, by Leon Podles. The other books that attempt to address why men shun church the way Rosie avoids a string bikini have nothing on this bad boy. This book dissects the dilemma of men dissing church better than any book on the planet. Podles shows how it happened, when it happened and what to do about it. This book is a wrecking crane to effeminate and crippled Christianity. Buy one for your pastor, and then pray he implements what lies within.

Ruling in Babylon: Seven Habits of Highly Effective Twentysomethings, by me, Doug Giles (Y'know I had to shamelessly plug at least one of my own books). This compilation of twenty-seven scripts from my radio show is for twentysomethings who are sick of picking lint from their navels while the secular regressives systematically take over our nation. I show in a scant 116 pages what caused the prophet Daniel and his three compadres to influence a crappy environment 2,600 years ago. Buy a stack of them and hand them out to your church's college students and let the revolution begin.

Prophetic Untimeliness: A Challenge to the Idol of Relevance, by Os Guinness. Never have Christians tried to be so relevant. But never have Christians ended up so irrelevant. How can this be? The problem, says Os Guinness, is that our views of relevance and our efforts to redefine ourselves are captive to the seductions and pressures of our modern clock culture. Ironically, we end up as neither relevant nor faithful. And in the process we are in danger of losing not only our identity but our authority, our significance, and even our very soul. *Prophetic Untimeliness* is a hard-hitting critique written with deep love for the church. It offers constructive suggestions for living with integrity in the midst of modern pressures and explores how to be truly relevant without being trivial or trendy. (From the back cover)

The Serrated Edge: A Brief Defense of Biblical Satire and Trinitarian Skylarking, by Doug Wilson. Satire is a kind of preaching. Satire pervades Scripture. Satire treats the foibles of sinners with a less than perfect tenderness. But, if a Christian employs satire today, he is almost immediately called to account for his "unbiblical" behavior. Yet Scripture shows that the central point of some religious controversies is to give offense. When Christ was confronted with ecclesiastical obstinacy and other forms of arrogance, he showed us a godly pattern for giving offense. In every controversy, godliness and wisdom (or the lack of them) are to be determined by careful appeal to the Scriptures and not to the fact of someone having taken offense. Perhaps they ought to have taken offense, and perhaps someone ought to have endeavored to give it (from Canon Press). Doug Wilson shows the Christian how to serve a nice satirical slice of sardonic pie to the willfully impenitent in this blistering read. Tasty.

Defending Your Faith: An Introduction to Apologetics, by Dr. R. C. Sproul. There is a widespread belief that reason and faith are incompatible and opposed to each other. Faith is viewed as subjective, emotional, a crutch for those who find the real world too hard. Though many of the world's finest minds hold this view, the Bible teaches that it is the fool who says there is no God. Sproul clearly and simply argues that at its core Christianity is rational. He focuses on defending the basic truth claims for two of the most crucial issues of apologetics: God's existence and the Bible's authority. In this primer of apologetic thought, Dr. Sproul affirms four logical principles that are necessary for all real discussion and teaches you how to defend your faith in a faithless world. Using the writings of church fathers and philosophers throughout the ages, he uncovers the common ideologies that work against faith. The defense of the faith is not a luxury or an intellectual vanity. It is a task appointed by God that you should be able to give a reason for the hope that is in you as you bear witness before the world. (from Amazon.com)

The Christian In Complete Armour, by William Gurnall. Gurnall's *The Christian in Complete Armour* is one of the classic Puritan books on practical spiritual warfare and how it plays out in daily living. John Newton said that if he might read only one book besides the Bible he would choose *The Christian in Complete Armour.* This book is a veritable battery for the believer intent upon putting a deep gaping wound in Satan's crumbling kingdom.

Why Revival Tarries, by Leonard Ravenhill. If the Christian really wants to change our nation then prayer for reformation needs to be on his to-do list. My old mentor Leonard Ravenhill lines out in this eyebrow-melting tome what happens to a nation when believers stop merely blathering on about how bad it is and hit their knees in prayer.

All of the above make up a high protein, low fat meat feast that I guarantee will set the Christian on course to be a massive disaster to el Diablo and his defeated minions. Now, go to Amazon.com, click your mouse, melt your plastic and make 2008 the year of crazy-over-the-top-insane growth for Christ and His kingdom.

Appendix:

The Cultural Acid Test for Pastors

The way I see it, the "God job" has two fronts: 1) to reach out to a lost soul helping to keep it from hell and 2) to righteously leaven our current cruddy culture for Christ.

First, Pastors and Priests are to study and teach the word of God carefully and apply it to our lives practically, so we don't end up drinking goofy grape and committing suicide en masse with the latest Jim Jones cult. Additionally, they are called to help their congregants build the good society in our nation. Y'know, the "Thy will be done on earth as it is in heaven" stuff?

A minister has the responsibility of massive influence woven into his job. Instead of using it to fleece his sheep, to molest altar boys, or simply to dole out clichés like a drugged up James Blunt, why not re-align with Scripture and focus on fixing this mucked up culture? Huh?

This means you must not focus your attention only on evangelism but also weigh in on all things which affect our culture, e.g, business, entertainment, education and yes, politics. All the aforementioned directly affect the health and wealth of the people you are trying to reach; and they require that you have a biblically based opinion on each category in order to influence them in ways that honor God.

Given that this is an election year and that the culture-dividing issues are more obvious than Pam Anderson's "upgraded" breast implants, it is mind-boggling that many clergy are mute or side with parties, policies and principles that are antithetical to what Scripture clearly states is holy, just and good. As far as I'm concerned, a silent or waffling pastor or priest in today's climate is a bad guy. I don't care how much he likes kitty cats and candy canes. Look, mute boy, if you're not in the middle of this crucial cultural squabble, then you're Dr. Evil in my book.

In some kind of ascending order, it seems to me there are 10 reasons why pastors and priests avoid political issues and why they are chicken hearted.

1. Fear of man. If you purport to be a man of "the cloth," then your regard for God and His opinion must trump the trepidation of the creature God created from spit and mud. Come on, man of God, don't fear us. We're ants with cell phones that'll shoot Botox into our foreheads. We're friggin' weird and fickle weather vanes of the modern media. Lead us . . . don't follow us!

Never live for a nod from the congregation or some political twerp or a particular party, especially when said group is way off biblical base.

2. Ignorance. Most people are not bold in areas where they are ignorant . . . always excepting Nancy Pelosi, of course. I know keeping up with all the pressing political issues is maddening, but that's life, Dinky; and if you want to be a voice in society and not just an echo, you have got to be in the know. Staying briefed, running each political issue through the gauntlet of Scripture and determining God's mind on a certain subject are par for the course for the hardy world changer. It's the information age. Get informed and watch your boldness increase.

3. Division. Y'know, I hate the current non-essential divisions in the church as much as the next acerbic Christian

columnist. Squabbling over the color of the carpet, who'll play the organ next Sunday or who is the Beast of Revelation, is stupidity squared. Hey, divisive Christian rebel without a clue—get a life, por favor! Or become a Satanist and go screw up their church. Do something other than make mountains out of your little molehill issues.

That being said, however, there's a time and place for a biblical throw-down and an ecclesiastical split from political policies and parties:

- When the taking of an unborn life is the issue.
- When marriage is being redefined.
- When runaway judges are attempting to expunge God and His law from our country's national life.

For a minister to seek unity with secularists when they are trashing and rewriting scripture with impunity is to side with evil and to allow darkness to succeed. On these kinds of issues, the minister cannot group hug the secular or quasi-Christian thugs.

4. Last Days Madness. Many ministers do not get involved in political issues because they believe that "it simply doesn't matter" since "the end has come," and Jehovah is about to run the credits on this failed earth flick. These defeatists believe that any change in the jet stream, war, earthquakes, a warming globe, the success of a corrupt politician—even a new Shakira video—are "proof" that God is getting really, really ticked off, and that His only recourse is to have Christ physically return and kick some major butt.

They see the church and themselves as impotent and having no real ability to change things culturally with any long range ramifications. Thus, any stab at a better tomorrow is simply an exercise in futility for this crew. Attempting to right culture is, in their eyes, equivalent to polishing brass on a sinking ship; therefore, they are content to simply pass out tracts, tramp from Christian rock concert to Christian rock concert, eat fatty foods and stare at Christian TV.

5. Sloth. Classically defined, sloth is lethargy stemming from a sense of hopelessness. Viewing our nation and the world as an irreparable disaster, where our exhortations, prayers, votes and labors will not produce any temporal fruit, leaves one with all the fervor of a normal guy who's forced to French kiss his sister.

If you're wondering why your flock is so apathetic, Pastor Grim Carnage, ask yourself if you have stolen their earthly hope that their valiant efforts can actually prevail in time, and not just in eternity? If you constantly pump the doom and gloom message, if you teach them that evil will ultimately triumph on our terra firma, if you spew messages that consciously or unconsciously convey "big, anti-Christ" and "little Jesus Christ," then you have effectively zapped what's left of your parishioners' passion.

6. They don't want to lose their Tax Exempt status. Many pastors, priests and parishioners have been cowed into inactivity by the threatened loss of their tax-exempt status if they say anything remotely political. This can make pastors who don't, or won't, get good legal advice about as politically active as Howard Hughes was during the flu season.

The church may, among other things, register their members to vote, pass out voter guides, invite all candidates in a race to speak (even if only one of them shows up) and speak directly about specific issues.

Off the clock, in his personal capacity, the pastor or priest can endorse and support (or oppose) whomever or whatever he wishes—like any other citizen. There are no limitations to the individual; the ones that do exist under the 501(c)(3) statute are only for the church entity and/or the pastor in his official capacity, not for the pastor or the members who make up the church.

The Cultural Acid Test for Pastors

7. They bathe in paltry pietism. Pastors and priests avoid politics because such concerns are "unspiritual," and their focus is on the "spirit world." Yes, to such imbalanced ministers, political affairs are seen as "temporal and carnal," because pastors and priests trade in the "eternal and spiritual," such "transient" issues get the same attention from them as Rosie's AbBlaster does from her.

This bunch is primarily into heavenly emotions and personal Bible study, and they stay safely tucked away from society and its complicated issues. They forget that they are commanded to be seriously engaged with our culture.

8. They have bought into the Taliban comparison. Pastors and priests have muffled their political voices because they fear being lumped in with Islam by the politically correct thought police. The correlation made between Christians' non-violent attempts at policy persuasion and the Taliban's kill-you-in-your-sleep campaigns is nothing more than pure, uncut crapola.

Ministers, please blow off the tongue-wagging blowhards who try to intimidate you into silence by making quantum, ludicrous, scat-laden and analogous leaps in equating the implementation of a gracious, Biblical worldview with the Islam-o-fascists cross-eyed perspective.

9. They can't say, "Heck no!" to minutiae. Some ministers can't get involved in studying or speaking out regarding pressing issues simply because of the ten tons of junk they are forced to field within their congregations. Spending time wet nursing 30-year-olds without a life and being bogged down in committee meetings over which shade of pink paint should be used for the Women Aglow's ministerial wing of their church, ministers are lucky if they get to study the Bible nowadays—much less anything else.

This is the fault of both the ministers with their messiah complexes and the congregants with their me-monkey syndromes, and they must all have an exorcism (or something) if the church is going to tackle cultural issues.

10. They likey the money. The creepy thing about a lot of ministers is their unwillingness to give political or cultural offense when offense is needed, simply because taking a biblical stand on a political issue might cost them their time-share in Sanibel and their 550i. Oh well, what do you expect? Christ had His Judas, and evangelicalism has it cheap hookers.

Never fear, pastor. Even though nailing your colors to the mast during putrid political times might cost you a parishioner or two, don't sweat it. There are also tens of thousands of serious parishioners who are looking for leaders with the guts to lead the church to make its proper stance during the days of Madonna, Ward Churchill and Osama.

If the ministers within the good old US of A would crucify their fear of man, get solidly briefed regarding the chief political issues, not sweat necessary division, not get caught up in last days madness, maintain their hope for tomorrow, understand their liberties under God and our Constitution, not become so heavenly minded that they're no earthly good, focus on the majors and blow off bowing to cash instead of convictions, then maybe . . . just maybe . . . we will see their influence cause our nation to take a righteous turn away from the secularist progressives' putrid pit.

About the Author

Doug Giles is the creator and host of ClashRadio.com, a winner of seven Silver Microphone Awards and two Communicator Awards.

In addition, Doug is a popular columnist, minister and award-winning writer. His column is read worldwide each week on the nation's largest conservative news portal, TownHall.com.

His articles have been taken up by several other print and online news sources, including *The Washington Times* and *ABC News,* and he is a regular guest on both major television and nationally syndicated radio news programs across the nation.

Giles is also the mad man behind *ClashTV*, which features Doug's cultural commentary put to film.

Giles earned his Bachelor of Fine Arts degree from Texas Tech University and studied for his Master of Arts in Christianity and Culture from Knox Theological Seminary.

He's the author of five books, *Ruling in Babylon: Seven Habits of Highly Effective Twentysomethings* (2003); *Political Twerps, Cultural Jerks, Church Quirks* (2004); *The Bulldog Attitude: Get It or Get Left Behind* (2006); *10 Habits of Decidedly Defective People: The Successful Loser's Guide to Life* (2007) and this one: *A Time to Clash: Papers from a Provocative Pastor (2008).*

For more information regarding Doug Giles or to contact him, log onto ClashRadio.com or call 786.28Clash.

Printed in the United States
208942BV00001B/409/A